Accounting for Climate Resilience in Infrastructure Investment Decisionmaking

A Data-Driven Approach for Department of the Air Force Project Prioritization

ANU NARAYANAN, SCOTT R. STEPHENSON, MICHAEL T. WILSON,
MARIA MCCOLLESTER, SARAH WEILANT, EMMI YONEKURA,
SASCHA ISHIKAWA, JAY BALAGNA, KRISTA ROMITA GROCHOLSKI,
NIHAR CHHATIAWALA

Prepared for the Department of the Air Force
Approved for public release; distribution is unlimited.

RAND PROJECT AIR FORCE

For more information on this publication, visit **www.rand.org/t/RRA1730-1**.

About RAND

The RAND Corporation is a research organization that develops solutions to public policy challenges to help make communities throughout the world safer and more secure, healthier and more prosperous. RAND is nonprofit, nonpartisan, and committed to the public interest. To learn more about RAND, visit www.rand.org.

Research Integrity

Our mission to help improve policy and decisionmaking through research and analysis is enabled through our core values of quality and objectivity and our unwavering commitment to the highest level of integrity and ethical behavior. To help ensure our research and analysis are rigorous, objective, and nonpartisan, we subject our research publications to a robust and exacting quality-assurance process; avoid both the appearance and reality of financial and other conflicts of interest through staff training, project screening, and a policy of mandatory disclosure; and pursue transparency in our research engagements through our commitment to the open publication of our research findings and recommendations, disclosure of the source of funding of published research, and policies to ensure intellectual independence. For more information, visit www.rand.org/about/research-integrity.

RAND's publications do not necessarily reflect the opinions of its research clients and sponsors.

About This Report

The research reported here was commissioned by the Air Force Director of Civil Engineers, Deputy Chief of Staff for Logistics, Engineering and Force Protection, Headquarters U.S. Air Force, and conducted within the Resource Management Program of RAND Project AIR FORCE (PAF) as part of a fiscal year 2022 project, "Building Resilience to Natural Hazards."

In fiscal year 2020, RAND PAF conducted analysis that provided an enterprisewide view of the Department of the Air Force's (DAF's) installation exposure to natural hazards.[1] That project's research outputs included an initial characterization of the exposure of continental United States DAF installations to a select set of hazards, an approach to compare the costs of proactive investments in infrastructure resilience with costs of rebuilding postdisaster, and a method for considering hazard seasonality in continuity of operations planning. That work did not address related questions of how to identify projects that might improve installation resilience, how to characterize the resilience benefits afforded by proposed projects, and how to compare those benefits across projects to inform the prioritization process.

This project builds on that prior effort to support these needs and aims to improve the DAF's ability to prioritize installation projects that would enhance resilience to climate-driven natural hazards. DAF infrastructure planning and resourcing processes do not explicitly account for climate resilience. This report provides the DAF with a structured framework for screening infrastructure projects based on their potential climate resilience value so that investment decisions may credibly and systematically consider climate-related risk and resilience at the enterprise level. We hope that this work will be of use to those in the DAF who support installation planning efforts, requirements identification and project submissions, project prioritization, review and validation, and resource allocation. Specifically, in addition to the sponsor, this work should be of value to those within the Office of the Secretary of the Air Force, Energy, Installations, and Environment (SAF/IE) with oversight of Air Force installation programs, staff at the Air Force Civil Engineer Center (AFCEC), the Air Force Installation and Mission Support Center (AFIMSC), and DAF installations.

RAND Project AIR FORCE

RAND Project AIR FORCE (PAF), a division of the RAND Corporation, is the Department of the Air Force's (DAF's) federally funded research and development center for studies and

---

[1] Anu Narayanan, Michael J. Lostumbo, Kristin Van Abel, Michael T. Wilson, Anna Jean Wirth, and Rahim Ali, *Grounded: An Enterprise-Wide Look at Department of the Air Force Installation Exposure to Natural Hazards: Implications for Infrastructure Investment Decisionmaking and Continuity of Operations Planning*, RAND Corporation, RR-A523-1, 2021.

analyses, supporting both the United States Air Force and the United States Space Force. PAF provides the DAF with independent analyses of policy alternatives affecting the development, employment, combat readiness, and support of current and future air, space, and cyber forces. Research is conducted in four programs: Strategy and Doctrine; Force Modernization and Employment; Resource Management; and Workforce, Development, and Health. The research reported here was prepared under contract FA7014-22-D-0001.

Additional information about PAF is available on our website: www.rand.org/paf/.

This report documents work originally shared with the DAF on September 9, 2022. The draft report, dated September 2022, was reviewed by formal peer reviewers and DAF subject-matter experts.

Acknowledgments

We are grateful to Brig Gen William Kale and his successor, Brig Gen Brian Hartless, for their support of the work. We are also grateful to David Carter, the action officer, and Lt Col Phillip Baker for their guidance throughout the course of the project. We also would like to thank various people across the Air Force, including personnel at Langley and Beale Air Force bases, AFCEC, AFIMSC, and the Office of the Deputy Assistant Secretary of the Air Force (Installations), for engaging with the project team and providing data and information needed to complete our analysis. We are also grateful to Stephanie Young and Anna Jean Wirth of the RAND Corporation for their program leadership.

Summary

Issue

Climate-driven natural hazards will continue to affect Department of the Air Force (DAF) installations and missions for the foreseeable future. There is a need for the DAF to consider how installation infrastructure projects that improve hazard resilience may be prioritized among all projects under consideration for funding. Although the DAF is taking initial steps to integrate hazard resilience into its existing funding and evaluation processes, DAF processes for allocating funds for infrastructure generally do not account for system performance under different threats and hazards.

Approach

Informed by reviews of relevant DAF and U.S. Department of Defense (DoD) policy and guidance documents and interviews with select DAF stakeholders and subject-matter experts (SMEs), we identified a way to compare infrastructure projects based on their ability to improve installation resilience to climate-related hazards. We developed a four-step approach that the DAF could implement (using largely available data) to screen infrastructure projects on the basis of their potential to enhance installation climate resilience. We also undertook a review of other organizations' approaches to climate resilience investment decisionmaking to understand how other organizations approach this challenge, and we provide the DAF with suggestions on how it might structure its own processes moving forward. From this review and insights obtained from DAF policy and guidance documents, interviews with DAF personnel, and our experience applying our own framework to a variety of sample resilience projects, we offer several findings and recommendations for the DAF.

Key Findings

- A review of DAF documents provided detailed and grounded understanding of policy and guidance regarding resilience, clarifying the roles of organizations that lead climate-related efforts relevant to installations. Additional review of resilience definitions and existing frameworks (e.g., the Resilience Dividend Valuation Model) provided a basis for the structure of our framework.
- Interviews with key DAF stakeholders and SMEs confirmed the need for a systematic framework for comparing and prioritizing projects based on their climate resilience value.
- Our review of other organizations' approaches to climate resilience investment decisionmaking revealed common practices and process elements, which largely align with key components of our proposed framework and further support the potential efficacy of such an approach. Similar to the DAF, our comparison federal agencies are

primarily in the development and evaluation phases of their climate risk assessment processes, whereas private-sector organizations have incorporated climate into their environmental, social, and governance considerations within their standard risk management processes.

- Climate uncertainty presents a key challenge for resilience planning and investment. Therefore, considerations of uncertainty must be integrated into any prioritization of resilience investments.

Recommendations

- **The DAF should use a systematic approach to compare projects with either an explicit or implicit climate resilience focus.** The presented framework facilitates the comparison of projects with either an *explicit* or *implicit* climate resilience focus by enumerating (and, where possible, quantifying) their potential benefits as measured by multiple metrics. The framework is intended to serve as an initial screening tool with additional local analyses guiding project prioritization and funding decisions.
- **To implement the presented framework, the DAF will need to**
    - **Identify specific steps in existing or anticipated project planning, prioritization, and validation processes where such a framework would be most useful;** for example, requirements identification and project submission (primarily by installations), project prioritization (at the installation and major command levels), review and validation of projects (by the Air Force Civil Engineer Center [AFCEC] or Air Force Installation and Mission Support Center), and development of installation climate resilience plans (by installations and AFCEC).
    - **Identify project pools within which the framework might be applied.** For instance, projects could be screened in advance of applying the framework to evaluate only projects with comparable (high) costs or those projects that are tagged as having resilience value in AFCEC's military construction (MILCON) integrated priority list (IPL) tool (discussed in Chapter 2).
    - **Compile, adapt, or generate data and information needed to evaluate projects using the framework and identify appropriate entities for carrying out each step.** Much of the data requisite for implementing the framework can be generated centrally (e.g., by AFCEC) and ahead of time. For instance, the first step of characterizing the baseline exposure of installation assets (described in Chapter 3) does not require knowledge of specific projects and can be completed ahead of time by a team of analysts with access to the types of centralized datasets that we describe throughout this report.
    - **Create concrete methods to inject relevant data into processes.** For instance, information could be integrated into planning platforms or portals that AFCEC maintains to facilitate more-efficient application of the framework.
    - **Account for climate uncertainty throughout.** Those implementing the framework should consider multiple climate scenarios in estimations of baseline exposure and exposure reductions. Robust and adaptive strategies should be favored over those optimized for present conditions only.

Contents

Figures and Tables

Figures

Tables

Chapter 1. Introduction

Climate-driven natural hazards are and will remain a perennial threat to the Department of the Air Force's (DAF's) installations and missions for the foreseeable future. The diversity of geographic environments in which the DAF must operate, within the continental United States (CONUS) and around the world, means that DAF bases are regularly at risk of exposure to numerous hazards with potential to affect missions in a variety of ways. Hazard exposure impacts range from temporary disruption of non–mission-essential operations, such as the evacuation of Travis Air Force Base (AFB) because of wildfires in 2020,[1] to catastrophic damage requiring full-scale repair and rebuilds, exemplified by the $4.7 billion of damage caused by Hurricane Michael at Tyndall AFB in 2018.[2] Although not all hazards are driven by long-term climate change, there is clear scientific evidence that global warming exacerbates the environmental conditions under which wildfires, severe storms, and other hazard events are likely to occur. This climate-driven enhanced risk environment, with increased hazard incidence and/or severity, is likely to persist in the coming decades as global anthropogenic greenhouse gas (GHG) emissions are projected to increase at least through 2050,[3] threatening to degrade infrastructure across the United States throughout the 21st century.[4]

U.S. Department of Defense (DoD) and DAF policy and guidance discuss past and ongoing threats to installations from natural hazards, many of which are expected to increase in severity and frequency because of climate change. Congress, through the National Defense Authorization Act, has required DoD services to examine the climate vulnerability of installations since fiscal year (FY) 2018, and, in FY20, it updated requirements to improve installation resilience to specific hazards, including extreme weather events, sea level rise, wildfire, and flooding.[5] The 2021 *Department of Defense Climate Adaptation Plan* articulated several lines of effort to

---

[1] Diana Stancy Correll, "Travis Air Force Base Orders Evacuations Following LNU Lightning Complex Fire," *Air Force Times*, August 20, 2020.

[2] Joe Gould, "Storm-Ravaged Bases Wait on Washington for Repair Money," *Defense News*, May 10, 2019.

[3] Intergovernmental Panel on Climate Change (IPCC), "Summary for Policymakers," in V. Masson-Delmotte, P. Zhai, A. Pirani, S. L. Connors, C. Péan, S. Berger, N. Caud, Y. Chen, L. Goldfarb, M. I. Gomis, M. Huang, K. Leitzell, E. Lonnoy, J. B. R. Matthews, T. K. Maycock, T. Waterfield, O. Yelekçi, R. Yu, and B. Zhou, eds., *Climate Change 2021: The Physical Science Basis*, Cambridge University Press, 2021.

[4] U.S. Global Change Research Program (USGCRP), *Fourth National Climate Assessment Impacts, Risks, and Adaptation in the United States*, Vol. II, 2018.

[5] Council on Strategic Risks and the Center for Climate and Security, *Climate Change and the National Defense Authorization Act*, June 2022; Anu Narayanan, Michael J. Lostumbo, Kristin Van Abel, Michael T. Wilson, Anna Jean Wirth, and Rahim Ali, *Grounded: An Enterprise-Wide Look at Department of the Air Force Installation Exposure to Natural Hazards: Implications for Infrastructure Investment Decisionmaking and Continuity of Operations Planning*, RAND Corporation, RR-A523-1, 2021.

accelerate adaptation to climate impacts, including an intent to increase built and natural installation infrastructure resilience through comprehensive installation assessment, progress and performance tracking, and improved building standards to account for altered future climate conditions (Line of Effort 3).[6] Furthermore, the plan's first line of effort directs services to explicitly incorporate climate exposure and performance metrics into cost-benefit analysis and data analytics at the enterprise level with the aim of informing long-term resourcing and budgetary decisionmaking. DoD has also invested in improving understanding of installations' exposure through the DoD Climate Assessment Tool (DCAT). Built on an existing Army tool (ACAT), the DCAT provides screening-level assessments of projected future exposure from eight hazards at 1,055 installations across DoD.[7]

The DAF's efforts to improve understanding of and resilience to climate risks at installations align with these departmentwide objectives. Recent revisions to Air Force Instruction (AFI) 32-1015, the policy document that establishes a comprehensive and integrated planning framework for development and redevelopment of Air Force installations, includes planning guidance for overall resilience to severe weather and climate hazards, as well as specific guidance related to floodplains and sea level rise.[8] In addition, the 2020 *Air Force Civil Engineer Severe Weather/Climate Hazard Screening and Risk Assessment Playbook* (commonly referred to as the Severe Weather Playbook [SWP]), developed in response to a DAF mandate to consider severe weather and climate risk in Installation Development Plans (IDPs) and facility projects, provides installation personnel with a systematic self-assessment framework to screen and assess current and future risk of exposure to a variety of hazards. It establishes a minimum screening list of severe weather and climate phenomena, provides guidance to determine the level of exposure, and outlines initial steps for how installations may integrate assessment outputs into existing plans and processes.[9] The 2022 DAF *Climate Action Plan* establishes a goal of fully implementing the SWP by FY26, in addition to increasing overall investments in base resilience to $100 million per year by FY27.[10] Outputs from the SWP are also expected to inform forthcoming Installation Climate Resilience Plans (ICRPs) now mandated by Congress as a part of IDPs. The ICRPs will include overviews of hazard risks and threats, vulnerable assets or

---

[6] DoD, *Department of Defense Climate Adaptation Plan*, September 1, 2021.

[7] A. O. Pinson, K. D. White, E. E. Ritchie, H. M. Conners, and J. R. Arnold, *DoD Installation Exposure to Climate Change at Home and Abroad*, U.S. Army Corps of Engineers, April 2021.

[8] AFI 32-1015, *Integrated Installation Planning*, Department of the Air Force, July 30, 2019, corrective action, January 4, 2021.

[9] Office of the Director of Civil Engineers, "Directorate of Civil Engineers Solicits Installation Assistance to Screen for Severe Weather/Climate Hazards on AF Installations," Headquarters Air Force, September 3, 2020.

[10] DAF, *Department of the Air Force Climate Action Plan*, Office of the Assistant Secretary for Energy, Installations, and Environment, October 2022b.

infrastructure, lessons learned from impacts from previous hazard events, and ongoing and planned projects to mitigate future impacts.[11]

Against this backdrop, and as revealed by our conversations with DAF stakeholders, there is a need to consider how installation infrastructure projects that improve hazard resilience may be prioritized among all projects under consideration for funding and how the resilience benefits afforded by one project may be evaluated against the resilience afforded by other projects. Although the DAF is taking initial steps to integrate hazard resilience into its existing project funding and evaluation processes, infrastructure funding processes generally do not account for system performance under different threats and hazards.[12] For example, projects funded through the Facilities Sustainment, Restoration, and Modernization (FSRM) account must undergo evaluation through the Air Force Comprehensive Asset Management Plan (AFCAMP) process, which, until recently, mainly considered the probability of failure (PoF) of relevant assets, the consequences of failure (CoF), and estimated life-cycle cost savings afforded by the project.[13] Recent changes to the AFCAMP business rules elevate the role of major command (MAJCOM) priority points to the primary determinant of a project's ability to compete in the evaluation cycle. Although MAJCOMs may choose to consider a project's resilience potential as a factor in their evaluation, there is no requirement to do so.[14] Similarly, projects considered for funding through the military construction (MILCON) and/or Unspecified Minor MILCON (UMMC) Working Group process may be tagged with a "resilience factor" indicating their relevance for one or more areas of resilience; however, there is no requirement to explicitly account for this factor in prioritization decisions (see Chapter 2).[15] Furthermore, there is currently no requirement or process to evaluate projects with the aim of selecting those projects that would collectively

---

[11] U.S. Code, Title 10, Armed Forces; Subtitle A, General Military Law; Part IV, Service, Supply, and Procurement; Chapter 169, Military Construction and Military Family Housing; Subchapter III, Administration of Military Construction and Military Family Housing; Section 2864, Master Plans for Major Military Installations.

[12] DoD defines *resilience* as the "ability to anticipate, prepare for, and adapt to changing conditions and withstand, respond to, and recover rapidly from disruptions" (DoD Directive [DoDD] 4715.21, *Climate Change Adaptation and Resilience*, U.S. Department of Defense, January 14, 2016). See also Narayanan et al., 2021.

[13] FSRM is part of the operation and maintenance appropriation. To obtain these funds, installation support organizations can submit projects through the AFCAMP process for consideration of centralized funds managed by the Air Force Installation and Mission Support Center (AFIMSC) and executed by the Air Force Civil Engineer Center (AFCEC). For further details, see Anu Narayanan, Debra Knopman, Kristin Van Abel, Benjamin M. Miller, Nicholas E. Burger, Martha Blakely, Alexander D. Rothenberg, Luke Muggy, and Patrick Mills, *Valuing Air Force Electric Power Resilience: A Framework for Mission-Level Investment Prioritization*, RAND Corporation, RR-2771-AF, 2019; Patrick Mills, Muharrem Mane, Kenneth Kuhn, Anu Narayanan, James D. Powers, Peter Buryk, Jeremy M. Eckhause, John G. Drew and Kristin F. Lynch, *Articulating the Effects of Infrastructure Resourcing on Air Force Missions: Competing Approaches to Inform the Planning, Programming, Budgeting, and Execution System*, RAND Corporation, RR-1578-AF, 2017.

[14] S. Bierman, B. Graf, and M. Akers, "CPI-Driven FY24 AFCAMP Business Rule Changes," Department of the Air Force briefing, 2022.

[15] AFCEC official, email, July 7, 2022.

reduce mission risks from exposure across the enterprise as a whole.[16] Anticipating exposure and planning for resilience are further complicated by uncertainties in the timing and magnitude of climate hazards and the degree to which these may change over time as climate change intensifies in the coming decades.[17]

In FY20, RAND Corporation Project AIR FORCE (PAF) researchers conducted an analysis that provided an enterprisewide view of DAF installation exposure to natural hazards.[18] Its research outputs were as follows: (1) an initial characterization of the exposure of CONUS Air Force installations to a select set of hazards, (2) an approach to compare the costs of proactive investments in infrastructure resilience with costs of rebuilding postdisaster, and (3) a method for considering hazard seasonality in continuity of operations planning. These outputs can be used to inform initial screening of installation exposure to prioritize where deeper-dive assessments should be conducted while also providing the DAF with information needed to decide how to allocate resilience resources and reduce mission risk across the enterprise.[19] However, that work did not address related questions of how to identify projects that might improve installation resilience, how to characterize the resilience benefits afforded by proposed projects, and how to compare those benefits across projects to inform the prioritization process. This project builds on that prior FY20 effort to support these needs.

Contributions of This Report

In this report, we aim to improve the DAF's ability to prioritize installation projects that would enhance resilience to climate-driven natural hazards. As noted above and detailed in Chapter 2, current DAF infrastructure planning and resourcing processes do not explicitly account for resilience to climate-driven hazards. This report provides the DAF with a structured framework for evaluating infrastructure projects based on their potential climate resilience value so that investment decisions may credibly and systematically consider climate-related risk and resilience at the enterprise level. Additional, deeper-dive analyses (e.g., of engineering constraints, project costs, or highly local hazard exposure patterns) that augment framework outputs should ultimately guide prioritization and funding decisions.

Although we developed the proposed framework with enterprise-level decisions in mind, we hope that this work will inform climate resilience-related project prioritization decisions

---

[16] AFIMSC official, interview with authors, February 23, 2022.

[17] Michelle E. Miro, Andrew Lauland, Rahim Ali, Edward W. Chan, Richard H. Donohue, Liisa Ecola, Timothy R. Gulden, Liam Regan, Karen M. Sudkamp, Tobias Sytsma, Michael T. Wilson, and Chandler Sachs, *Assessing Risk to the National Critical Functions as a Result of Climate Change*, Homeland Security Operational Analysis Center operated by the RAND Corporation, RR-A1645-7, 2022.

[18] Narayanan et al., 2021.

[19] Narayanan et al., 2021.

throughout the DAF's current processes. In the concluding chapter of this report, we identify sample decision points where a framework such as the one we propose might be used.

We recognize that not all projects that improve hazard resilience at installations will be explicitly identified as *resilience projects*. Some projects, such as the building of new infrastructure to replace an older facility, may improve resilience simply by virtue of the new infrastructure being built to a design standard higher than that of the facility it replaced, potentially enabling it to avoid or withstand more-severe or -prolonged exposure. Such projects, despite offering incidental resilience benefits, run the risk of having their climate resilience value overlooked if installations begin to prioritize resilience-oriented projects. Thus, the DAF needs a prioritization method that can identify potential resilience benefits in any proposed project, regardless of whether it is explicitly identified as such. The framework presented here facilitates direct comparison of projects with either an *explicit* or *incidental* climate resilience focus by enumerating (and where possible, quantifying) their potential benefits according to multiple metrics. In either case, the framework stops short of comparing a project's climate resilience benefits against other objectives and priorities it may address. In addition, we recognize that a resilience project may be designed to reduce installation exposure to hazards, reduce the vulnerability of specific installation assets to hazard exposure, or both. Our framework focuses on the first of these types of projects to align with the types of projects installation personnel highlighted in our discussions with them, such as relocating assets out of the floodplain and building perimeters to limit wildfire exposure.[20] Our framework incorporates information about the design standard of exposed buildings to illustrate one way in which vulnerability could be assessed in our framework, given the availability of appropriate metrics.

Finally, the presented framework aims to elucidate the relative *effectiveness* (measured in terms of possible mission impact and monetary losses) of proposed projects. There are two other key elements of resilience investment decisionmaking that the presented framework does not cover—the *costs* and *risks* (physical or programmatic) of candidate resilience measures. Decisionmaking regarding investments in installation resilience, whether to climate change or some other threat, will necessarily consider the relative costs of available options and the risks that are inherent to their implementation. The approach we present seeks only to make clear the resilience enhancement potential of projects, an attribute that can be difficult to define and one that will need to be weighed against other important considerations before any funding decisions are made.

Organization of the Rest of This Report

In Chapter 2, we present the results from a review of DAF and DoD documents and a series of interviews with DAF personnel. Through these combined tasks, we aimed to (1) identify DAF

---

[20] Langley AFB official, interview with authors, April 1, 2022.

analytic needs relevant to climate-related risks to infrastructure and (2) understand the extent to which current DAF processes for infrastructure planning, prioritizing, and resourcing account for climate resilience. We also present a review of commonly used conceptual frameworks for understanding resilience to provide context for our project prioritization framework.

In Chapter 3, we outline a data-driven, systematic approach for prioritizing climate resilience–related projects in four stages. We focus on two hazards that have potential to cause serious installation damage and mission disruption that are also projected to increase in frequency and/or severity as climate change worsens in the future: flooding and wildfire. The framework presents methods for characterizing asset exposure from these hazards at installations, approaches for identifying the *benefiting area* of proposed projects, metrics for quantifying the resilience benefits of projects within installations and across the enterprise, documentation of requisite data and information, and ways to compare projects based on their expected resilience benefits. Although the exposure analysis methodologies we use to demonstrate our framework are specific to flooding and wildfire, the framework could be applied to other hazards by substituting exposure analysis methodologies that capture or model the plausible extent and/or severity of those hazards.

Chapter 4 presents insights from a review of selected approaches to prioritizing investment in infrastructure resilience taken by five other organizations within DoD, the federal government, and the private sector. By examining how these organizations currently consider climate change in their infrastructure investment decisionmaking, we aim to identify recommendations for DAF process improvements that may complement insights obtained through application of the prioritization framework presented in Chapter 3.

In Chapter 5, we review key findings from our analysis and outlines several recommendations for integrating our proposed framework into existing DAF processes.

Chapter 2. Identifying DAF Analytic Needs for Climate Resilience Decisionmaking

In the previous chapter, we outlined the need for the DAF to use a systematic approach to prioritize investments in infrastructure and installation resilience to climate-driven natural hazards. In this chapter, we describe in greater detail three research efforts that helped establish that need and develop a basis for the framework described in Chapter 3—a review of relevant DAF and DoD policy documents, instructions, and directives; discussions with DAF representatives from various levels of the organization; and a review of existing frameworks for valuing resilience.

Document Review

We reviewed DAF and DoD policy, manuals, strategic plans, and Unified Facilities Criteria (UFC) to identify potentially relevant requirements, standards, and guidance for resilience-related decisionmaking and actions. In the review, we assessed stated responsibilities, resources, data, tools, and information available to the DAF and DoD that address or could address climate-related impacts on mission and/or installation facilities and assets. We also identified potential gaps in policy to reduce climate-related impacts to the DAF mission.

To limit the review to a period in which climate resilience would likely be discussed, we selected DoD and DAF documents, government reports, and other gray literature and academic research published since 2001. The following keywords were used to narrow the scope of relevant documents:

- "Air Force" OR "Department of Air Force" OR "DAF" OR "U.S. DAF" OR "U.S. Air Force*" OR "United States Air Force" OR "USAF" OR "United States Department of Defense" OR "Department of Defense" OR "DOD" OR "U.S. DOD" OR "DODM" OR "DODI" OR "DODD"
- "climate change" OR "climate-change" OR "defense infrastructure" OR "installation*" OR "military infrastructure" OR "resilien*" OR "climate resilien*" OR "disaster resilien*" OR "climate*" OR "climate crisis*" OR "installation assurance" OR "sustainab*" OR "crisis management" OR "natural disaster*" OR "energy management" OR "facilit*" OR "risk analys*" OR "system model*" OR "civil engineer*" OR "readiness" OR "environment*" OR "disaster*."

The search identified 163 documents that had a focus on installation exposure to natural hazards, mission impacts stemming from this exposure, and resilience options. Of the 163 documents, some were determined to be less relevant because of lack of detail or too a narrow or broad focus on ancillary topics, such as those found in congressional records and briefings, memos, and public laws. In all, we reviewed in detail 50 DAF and DoD documents comprising articles, fact sheets, policies, strategic plans, and UFCs. The following are examples of key policy documents that received a thorough review (for the full list, see the Document Review section in Appendix A):

- *Department of Defense Climate Adaptation Plan*
- *Department of Defense Climate Risk Analysis*[21]
- *Climate Change Adaptation and Resilience* (DoDD 4715.21)[22]
- *Mission Assurance* (DoDD 3020.40)[23]
- *Sustaining Access to the Live Training Domain* (Department of Defense Instruction [DoDI] 3200.21)[24]
- *Installation Energy Management* (DoDI 4170.11)[25]
- *Mission Sustainment* (Air Force Policy Directive [AFPD] 90-20)[26]
- *Mission Sustainment* (AFI 90-2001)[27]
- *Integrated Installation Planning* (AFI 32-1015)
- *Installation Master Planning* (UFC 2-100-01)[28]
- *Civil Engineering* (UFC 3-201-01).[29]

Among these documents, we identified the following types of plans as particularly relevant to installations, asset and resource management, and climate:

- Installation Energy Plan
- Installation Master Plan
- IDP
- ICRP
- Integrated Natural Resources Management Plan
- Comprehensive Asset Management Plan.

Our objective was not to examine resilience practices at specific installations but rather whether there were mechanisms within existing installation plan guidance at the enterprise level that would allow for the inclusion of climate resilience information relevant to installations.

---

[21] Office of the Undersecretary for Policy for Strategy, Plans, and Capabilities, *Department of Defense Climate Risk Analysis*, U.S. Department of Defense, October 2021.

[22] DoDD 4715.21, *Climate Change Adaptation and Resilience*, U.S. Department of Defense, January 14, 2016.

[23] DoDD 3020.40, *Mission Assurance*, U.S. Department of Defense, change 1, September 11, 2018.

[24] DoDI 3200.21, *Sustaining Access to the Live Training Domain*, U.S. Department of Defense, incorporating change 1, July 2, 2020.

[25] DoDI 4170.11, *Installation Energy Management*, U.S. Department of Defense, December 11, 2009.

[26] AFPD 90-20, *Mission Sustainment*, Department of the Air Force, April 18, 2019.

[27] AFI 90-2001, *Mission Sustainment*, Department of the Air Force, July 31, 2019.

[28] UFC 2-100-01, *Installation Master Planning*, U.S. Department of Defense, September 30, 2020, change 1, April 8, 2022.

[29] UFC 3-201-01, *Civil Engineering*, U.S. Department of Defense, December 20, 2022.

Document Review Conclusions

Our review revealed that different documents produced by different DAF and DoD organizations considered resilience to climate hazards in different ways. They also provided varying levels of detail for actions, responsibilities, and definitions of resilience. For example, some documents outlined explicit responsibilities of organizations and detailed the types of actions they should take. In other cases, documents offered more-general guidance about the types of roles and responsibilities needed to address resilience. The following list presents examples of required activities related to how installations can build resilience; the activities most relevant to resilience came from documents focused on installation planning, resource management, building sustainment, engineering, and mission sustainment:

- AFI 32-1015, Section 6.2.1.6—"Address energy and severe weather/climate resiliency in planning documents, including within district and component plans, in accordance with 10 USC § 2864. Plans shall identify facilities at risk (e.g., located in a current or potential future floodplain) or requiring additional resiliency measures."
- AFI 32-1015, Section 2.19.10.3—"Assess and manage risks associated with the effects of severe weather and a changing climate on built and natural infrastructure, in accordance with DoDD 4715.21, Climate Change Adaptation and Resilience."
- AFI 90-802, Section 3.3.2.1—"Assess Hazard Exposure. Evaluate the time, proximity, volume or repetition involved to determine the level of exposure to hazards."[30]
- Air Force Doctrine Publication (AFDP) 3-59—"Weather personnel routinely monitor weather along planned flight routes, alerting decision makers to the onset of hazardous weather conditions such as turbulence, icing, and thunderstorms."[31]

Although DoD and DAF guidance may be more general in terms of how DAF entities should incorporate climate resilience considerations, recent updates to DoD planning documents include directives to address climate more clearly and better standardize related terminology and activities across the services. For instance, 2022 revisions to UFC 2-100-01 updated planning processes and products to incorporate energy, climate, and military resilience and further standardized language regarding climate and weather considerations. The UFC also directs services to use the DCAT and the DoD Regional Sea Level Database to assist installations in identifying and planning for multiple climate scenarios.[32]

The document review provided detailed and grounded understanding of current policy and guidance, clarifying the roles of organizations that lead climate-related efforts relevant to such installations as AFCEC and AFIMSC. It also confirmed that further conversation with representatives from these organizations and from installations would be necessary to further

---

[30] AFI 90-802, *Risk Management*, Department of the Air Force, April 1, 2019.

[31] AFDP 3-59, *Weather Operations*, Curtis E. LeMay Center for Doctrine Development and Education, October 28, 2020.

[32] UFC 2-100-01, 2022; U.S. Climate Resilience Tool, "Department of Defense Regional Sea Level (DRSL) Database," webpage, last modified February 27, 2021.

capture the nuances between DAF policy and practice. In the next section, we describe insights gained from discussions with DAF representatives in detail.

Discussions with DAF Personnel

Building on the document review, we conducted seven interviews with individuals from across the DAF in consultation with our sponsor to better understand how they include climate change–related risks into their investment decisions for building installation resilience. We spoke with personnel from two main groups in the Air Force—those in headquarters-level installation support organizations (AFCEC and AFIMSC) and representatives from two installations. The DAF has 176 installations around the world, including active duty, Air National Guard, and Air Force Reserves. Although the framework we present in Chapter 3 could be applied to evaluate resilience projects at any DAF installation, the scope of this study afforded time for interviews with two installations only. We acknowledge that limiting engagement to two installations does not capture the diversity of missions or geography of DAF installations, which limits the degree to which our framework was informed directly by installation needs. However, the personnel at the installations with whom we spoke were identified by our sponsor as having particular insights relevant to natural hazard resilience. We sought information from personnel at AFCEC and AFIMSC pertaining to

- conceptualization and execution of existing installation project scoring models
- informational needs for incorporating considerations of climate resilience into existing scoring models and base-level climate related planning
- ongoing or planned enterprise-level initiatives for resilience investments.

We sought information from personnel at installations pertaining to

- climate-related risks that installations face
- processes and capabilities (tools, metrics, policies, data, or funds) for integrating climate hazard risk in installation planning
- links between installation exposure and mission risk
- ongoing, planned, or desired projects to improve hazard resilience at installations
- base-level information needs for climate-related planning and decisionmaking
- ongoing or planned projects to improve hazard resilience at installations.

We identified several roles and responsibilities in the policy documents pertaining to DAF policy and decisionmaking, as well as tactical actions and operations, that informed our list of interviewees. In particular, the roles listed in Table 2.1 emerged as critical (among others we were unable to directly engage) given they touch on elements of policy, project design, and execution, as described in AFI 32-1015.

Table 2.1. Relevant Roles in Installation Planning

Role	Stated Responsibilities
AFIMSC	2.16.1: "programming, budgeting, and funding the execution of Installation and Mission Support requirements, to include Program Objective Memorandum inputs for, validation of requirements, and advocacy to ensure continued installation operational capacity and capability for the enterprise."
AFCEC	2.17.1.3: "Execute Integrated Installation Planning programs (with the exception of Air Force Industrial Preparedness facilities)."
Installation commander	2.19.10.3: "Assess and manage risks associated with the effects of severe weather and a changing climate on built and natural infrastructure, in accordance with DoDD 4715.21, Climate Change Adaptation and Resilience."
Base civil engineer	2.32.5: "Execute installation development planning." 2.32.5.1: "Prepare, maintain and implement the Installation Development Plan." 2.32.5.2: "Collect, interpret, integrate, and present the vision of the Installation Commander and other senior installation leadership for mission requirements and installation development."

SOURCE: AFI 32-1015.

Ultimately, we held seven discussions with 16 DAF representatives from AFCEC and AFIMSC (spanning four directorates within) and from two installations: Beale AFB and Langley AFB. We chose these installations because each represented different assets and potential risks to mission if resilience is not accounted for; Langley AFB faces significant flood risk,[33] and Beale AFB is at risk of wildfire, flooding, and drought.[34] Our complete interview protocol is provided in Appendix B (see the "AFCEC/AFIMSC Interview Background and Questions" and "Installation Interview Background and Questions" sections).

DAF Discussion Insights

We discussed topics related to the identification, prioritization, funding, and complexity of climate resilience projects. The discussions highlighted a need for a systematic approach to identifying and understanding the value of infrastructure projects that may enhance installation resilience in a complex funding environment. Interviewees noted that DoD has implemented steps to understand the impacts of climate change and that efforts to address these impacts have been executed. For example, DoD conducted an audit to understand whether the services assessed and planned for installation facility resilience to climate change on installations in California, including those in the Air Force.[35]

---

[33] Amy Wagner, "Langley Construction FONPA Announcement," *Joint Base Langley-Eustis News*, July 18, 2011.

[34] Office of the Under Secretary of Defense for Acquisition and Sustainment, *Report on Effects of a Changing Climate to the Department of Defense*, U.S. Department of Defense, January 2019.

[35] Richard B. Vasquez, "Audit of Climate Change Adaptation and Facility Resilience at Military Installations in California," memorandum, December 6, 2021; Beale AFB official, interview with authors, April 18, 2022.

Project Scoring, Documentation, and Funding

Current processes for prioritizing infrastructure projects do not explicitly account for resilience. As part of the AFCAMP process, MAJCOMs may assign priority points to projects based on their mission impact. A MAJCOM may, therefore, allot priority points based on resilience at its discretion. This element of the scoring model is critical to a project's ability to compete for funding and will become even more so in the future with recent changes to AFCAMP business rules that elevated the significance of MAJCOM priority points above other scoring elements.[36] Currently, installations may improve a project's chances by submitting documentation that includes information on existing asset conditions and/or capabilities or benefits of the project that would support enterprise objectives or missions impact. Such aspects of projects may relate to resilience, such as providing redundant power in a facility, but how these attributes are linked to resilience may not be standard across projects.[37]

Under DAF processes, installation representatives communicate installation priorities in their project proposals for funding. Representatives may include resilience in those priorities and highlight them in project proposals. It is unclear whether there is a standardized way of noting resilience aspects in project submissions, making it difficult to readily identify climate factors or impacts in project proposal submissions. A DAF official noted that a natural order dictates which projects may be funded, starting with Tier 1 projects deemed critical to maintaining the enterprise mission.[38] However, this ordering may not reflect the second-order impacts or benefits, like those related to resilience, that other non–Tier 1 projects could provide.

Furthermore, funding that specifically targets resilience is limited. The FY23 DAF MILCON budget identifies a focus on critical infrastructure and building resilient facilities and infrastructure, totaling $2.3 billion,[39] but it is not further defined. Also, because funding for infrastructure projects often comes from FSRM accounts, which cover maintenance, financing resilience projects may present a trade-off to funding typical base maintenance. Another consideration offered by our interviewees was the need to secure more funding for personnel to support resilience projects. For example, if fire prevention and response facilities are determined to be a priority, enough people need to be staffed to handle the response, which one DAF official viewed as a more sustainable approach compared with employing individuals who may be deployed.[40]

---

[36] Bierman, Graf, and Akers, 2022.

[37] AFCEC official, interview with authors, February 25, 2022.

[38] Beale AFB official, interview with authors, April 18, 2022.

[39] DAF, *Fiscal Year 2023 Budget Overview*, March 28, 2022a.

[40] Beale AFB official, interview with authors, April 18, 2022.

Discussions with DAF personnel highlighted an ambiguity in DAF policy and guidance as to what constitutes a "resilience project," making it difficult to ensure that resilience effects are captured and taken into consideration when making funding decisions. For example, there are no criteria to determine whether a new building with updated engineering standards replacing an old building would be considered a resilience project, and if so, what those resilience benefits would be.[41] Another challenge is that there is no streamlined way to review the universe of known operational and mission failures that have already occurred as a result of asset degradation or failure (e.g., a broken heating, ventilation, and air conditioning system stopping pilots from flying).[42] As a result, capturing the benefits of resilience efforts, whether explicit or implicit, has proved difficult thus far.

The variation in project needs, and in the missions that installation assets support, creates challenges in determining what types of projects can be deemed related to climate resilience. DAF representatives highlighted several exacerbating factors to investment decisions, including the need to address both current climate issues (e.g., flooded roadways cutting off access to installations) and prevention planning for anticipated, longer-term effects (e.g., expected sea level rise, coastal resilience and infrastructure, and building or repairing dams for flood control).[43] Additionally, variation in climate threats and impacts presents challenges for decisionmakers as they consider and balance the needs of individual assets and the DAF infrastructure system by determining how and why to prioritize the resilience of one facility over another. For example, a minor resilience upgrade to a communications facility might be prioritized over a major upgrade to a horse stable because of the essential function that the communications facility provides to the installation.[44] These system-level complexities make it more difficult to understand how to define climate resilience projects, measure their impacts, and value their benefits or return on investment.

Furthermore, there is no single enterprisewide source that defines or outlines the characteristics of climate resilience projects.[45] However, project managers can tag some projects with a resilience factor that identifies aspects or attributes of resilience in AFCEC's MILCON integrated priority list (IPL) tool. MILCON business rules provide instructions on how to apply the resilience factors.[46] However, the factors are not used in prioritizing or scoring projects, nor have all prior projects been tagged in the IPL tool. Additionally, we are unaware of any similar

---

[41] AFCEC official, interview with authors, February 17, 2022.

[42] AFMISC official, interview with authors, February 28, 2022.

[43] AFCEC official, interview with the authors, February 17, 2022.

[44] Langley AFB official, interview with the authors, April 2, 2022.

[45] AFCEC official, interview with the authors, February 17, 2022.

[46] U.S. Air Force, *MILCON Business Rules*, version 1.1, May 2021, section A-2.3.29.

resilience factor tags for FSRM-funded projects. Identifying projects with a resilience factor tag stemmed from the desire to preidentify resilience-focused projects in the event that Congress decides to appropriate funds for such projects in the future. The following are four ways in which projects can be tagged with resilience factors in the IPL tool:[47]

- **Infrastructure resilience** addresses facility or other utility (nonenergy) vulnerabilities to an installation mission and increases the capability of the installation to avoid, prepare for, minimize the effect of, adapt to, and recover from extreme weather events.
- **Energy resilience** addresses energy and water vulnerabilities to an installation mission and increases the capability of the installation to avoid, prepare for, minimize the effect of, adapt to, and recover from extreme weather events.
- **Cybersecurity** addresses control system vulnerabilities to an installation mission and increases the capability of the installation to avoid, prepare for, minimize the effect of, adapt to, and recover from extreme weather events.
- **Emergency management** addresses other vulnerabilities in an installation's ability to prevent, mitigate, respond to, and recover from terrorist, manmade, and other (nonextreme weather) natural disasters.

Overall, our discussions with AFCEC, AFIMSC, and installation representatives helped us understand the DAF's processes for prioritization, where gaps in knowledge currently lie, and how and where a framework like the one we propose in Chapter 3 could be applied. Building on insights from these discussions, we then conducted a review of definitions and theories of resilience to understand how they might serve as a basis for a project prioritization framework for the DAF.

Toward a Resilience Framework for the DAF

Several resilience definitions and existing frameworks for understanding resilience aided the development of our framework presented in the next chapter (see the "Definitions and Concepts of Resilience" section in Appendix A for a list of definitions of resilience from this review). We focus on one, the Resilience Dividend Valuation Model (RDVM),[48] which provided a general approach for valuing resilience that we adapted for our own framework and also served as the theoretical basis for a derivative approach that influenced our framework.

---

[47] There is a fifth option in the drop-down menu called, "N/A—Resilience factor is not applicable." AFCEC official, email to authors, July 7, 2022.

[48] Craig A. Bond, Aaron Strong, Nicholas E. Burger, Sarah Weilant, Uzaib Saya, and Anita Chandra, *Resilience Dividend Valuation Model: Framework Development and Initial Case Studies*, RAND Corporation, RR-2129-RF, 2017. See also Craig A. Bond, Aaron Strong, Nicholas E. Burger, and Sarah Weilant, *Guide to the Resilience Dividend Valuation Model*, RAND Corporation, RR-2130-RF, 2017.

Definitions of Resilience

In the military, *resilience* is defined in multiple policy, strategy, and planning documents as "the ability to anticipate, prepare for, and adapt to changing conditions and withstand, respond to, and recover rapidly from disruptions."[49] The U.S. Air Force Strategic Plan describes resilience as the "ability of the Air Force units to continue to conduct air, space, and cyberspace operations despite disruption whether natural or man-made, inadvertent, or deliberate."[50] But these and other DAF resilience definitions do not explicitly include climate, despite the fact that climate is a major driver of several hazards with potential to disrupt mission operations. As climate change threatens to increase exposure to these hazards in the future, it is important that projects that aim to enhance long-term climate resilience be explicitly identified as such. Various resilience-related terms are defined in guidance documents that may touch on or address climate, including military installation resilience, resiliency, task-critical asset, climate change, energy and water resilience, hazards, adaptation, mitigation, and the attributes encompassed by the "Five Rs" of resilience: robustness, redundancy, resourcefulness, response, and recovery (see the "Definitions and Concepts of Resilience" section in Appendix A for a full list of terms).

Outside the military, definitions of resilience tend to focus on communities and individuals, and ecological, physical, and social systems.[51] Sample definitions include

- "the ability of social units to mitigate hazards"[52]
- "the capability to bounce back and use physical and economic resources effectively"[53]
- "[t]he ability . . . to deal with a state of continuous, long-term stress."[54]

Although we do not prescribe a specific definition of *resilience* in this report, we emphasize the "withstand" aspect of the definition included in DoDD 4715.21, used in multiple DoD documents, and broaden it to include reductions in exposure to climate-driven hazards. This approach is consistent with a risk-based approach to infrastructure management, as a system might be considered resilient if it is constructed or configured in such a way as to minimize its

---

[49] See AFI 32-1015 and Office of the Undersecretary for Policy for Strategy, Plans, and Capabilities, 2021.

[50] U.S. Air Force, *Strategic Posture Annex to the USAF Strategic Master Plan*, May 2015.

[51] See the "Definitions and Concepts of Resilience" section in Appendix A for a full list of definitions adapted from Fran H. Norris, Susan P. Stevens, Betty Pfefferbaum, Karen F. Wyche, and Rose L. Pfefferbaum, "Community Resilience as a Metaphor, Theory, Set of Capacities, and Strategy for Disaster Readiness," *American Journal of Community Psychology*, Vol. 41, Nos. 1–2, 2008.

[52] Michel Bruneau, Stephanie E. Chang, Ronald T. Eguchi, George C. Lee, Thomas D. O'Rourke, Andrei M. Reinhorn, Masanobu Shinozuka, Kathleen Tierney, William A. Wallace, and Detlof Von Winterfeldt, "A Framework to Quantitatively Assess and Enhance the Seismic Resilience of Communities," *Earthquake Spectra*, Vol. 19, No. 4, 2003.

[53] Douglas Paton and David Johnston, "Disasters and Communities: Vulnerability, Resilience and Preparedness," *Disaster Prevention and Management*, Vol. 10, No. 4, 2001.

[54] Michael Ganor and Yuli Ben-Lavy, "Community Resilience: Lessons Derived from Gilo Under Fire," *Journal of Jewish Communal Service*, Winter/Spring, 2003.

hazard exposure. A primary way in which (built or natural) infrastructure projects—the focus of this work—stand to enhance the DAF's climate resilience is by improving the ability of assets to withstand exposure to hazards or reducing exposure in the first place. Thus, we used this frame as a basis for identifying the types of projects that may build installations' resilience to climate impacts. We discuss this aspect of our framework in greater detail in the "Step 2—Identify the Project's Benefiting Area" section in Chapter 3.

Resilience Dividend Valuation Model

To set priorities among resilience projects, one must be able to evaluate the comparative benefits afforded by those projects. One way to conceive of the value of a resilience project is to consider its *resilience dividend*: "the difference in outcomes resulting from a resilience project compared to what those outcomes would have been without the resilience project."[55] The RDVM offers a framework for estimating the resilience dividend for a given project or policy that would enhance resilience (*intervention*) over a business-as-usual scenario. Its general approach is as follows:[56]

1. Define the intervention and business-as-usual scenarios.
2. Map (i.e., conceptualize) the system that the intervention is intended to benefit.
3. Define the shocks and/or stressors to the system.
4. Map out the changes to the system in the intervention and business-as-usual scenarios.
5. Estimate the intervention and business-as-usual paths.
6. Aggregate the estimates of well-being.

We adapt this general approach for the DAF context as follows:

1. Define the resilience project and business-as-usual (no project, or other [nonresilience] project) scenarios.
2. Map (i.e., define and geolocate) the set of installation assets that the project is intended to benefit.
3. Define the climate-driven hazards to which the assets may be exposed.
4. Conceptualize how hazard exposure may affect the assets under the project and business-as-usual scenarios.
5. Project the impact to installation and/or mission operations under the project and business-as-usual scenarios over time.
6. Calculate the benefits afforded by the project scenario over the business-as-usual scenario (i.e., the resilience dividend).

Following this adapted framework, Figure 2.1 illustrates the outcome of an investment in a resilience project in terms of this difference. The dividend, or the additional benefits or co-benefits afforded by a resilience project relative to a nonresilience project (business-as-usual), is represented by the space between the blue and purple lines. In the next chapter, we describe in

---

[55] Bond, Strong, Burger, Weilant et al., 2017, p. 2.

[56] Bond, Strong, Burger, Weilant et al., 2017, p. 19.

more detail the ways in which the resilience dividend and our adaptation of RDVM informed the development of our framework.

Figure 2.1. Schematic Representation of the Resilience Dividend

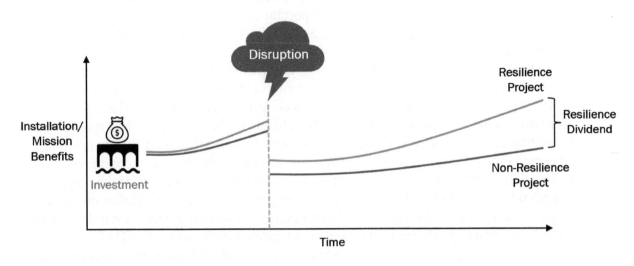

SOURCE: Adapted from Bond, Strong, Burger, Weilant et al., 2017.

Derivative Approaches to Valuing Resilience

In addition to reviewing the RDVM general approach, we examined three RDVM-like derivative tools and methods for guiding resilience project conception, design, and delivery for insights that could inform our framework: (1) Naval Facilities Engineering Systems Command's (NAVFAC's) *Climate Change Planning Handbook*,[57] (2) New York City Mayor's Office of Resiliency *Climate Resiliency Design Guidelines*,[58] and (3) the Federal Emergency Management Agency's (FEMA's) Building Resilient Infrastructure and Communities (BRIC) program.[59] Although two of these approaches (1 and 2) were determined to be insufficient to meet DAF needs, the third used a concept that directly informed a critical step of our framework.

1. In 2017, NAVFAC developed its *Climate Change Planning Handbook* to support installation planning and resilience that suggests ways to address resilience in four stages. Each stage includes multiple steps, such as determining asset scope, identifying and evaluating information, describing impacts, and developing a problem statement. Although this approach demonstrates the value of characterizing specific aspects of resilience projects and their benefits, our preliminary analysis indicated that using this approach would be too labor intensive to implement in the context of multiple hazards

---

[57] NAVFAC, *Climate Change Planning Handbook: Installation Adaptation and Resilience*, January 2017.

[58] New York City Mayor's Office of Resiliency, *Climate Resiliency Design Guidelines*, version 4, September 2020.

[59] FEMA, "Where Equity Fits into the BRIC/FMA Program Design and Community Resilience," BRIC and FMA Program Webinar Series, August 18, 2021c.

and across multiple installations—a critical feature of the framework we aimed to develop.

2. New York City's *Climate Resiliency Design Guidelines*, which were under development at the time of writing, focus on criticality and major projects and managing uncertainty. The guidelines highlight the importance of differentiating assets that benefit from a project by their value and function—an important consideration for the DAF. However, applying these guidelines in full requires a pilot effort to properly calibrate them, which was not feasible within the time frame of this study.

3. Launched in 2020, FEMA's BRIC program has distributed more than $1 billion in grants to state and local communities, tribes, and territories for hazard mitigation projects. This program applies to multiple natural hazards a concept derived from flood mitigation assistance grants that we found particularly valuable to the DAF's problem space—the benefiting area (see Chapter 3).[60] Using this method, subapplicants (the state or tribal government aggregates proposals and functions as the applicant) are encouraged to delineate (on a map or via detailed text description) where the benefits of the project are expected to fall. For example, a new fuels management strategy for wildfire might benefit an entire county, whereas a new stormwater pump station may account for only a small part of a community. This concept has a direct parallel in the context of DAF installations, as a given project might seek to (or incidentally) enhance resilience for a specific subset of geographically contiguous assets at an installation. As a program in active development and expansion, we recommend that the DAF continues to track the program's evolution, though it does have nuances, such as sociodemographic and geographic distribution concerns, that may not have an immediate parallel.[61] Furthermore, costing is an inherent part of the methodology, as are multiple rounds of state and technical expert review and scoring, which are likely beyond the scope and capabilities of the DAF at this time.[62]

Reviewing these approaches to operationalizing an RDVM-like framework provided valuable insights for developing a resilience valuation method that can leverage the datasets that the DAF has at its disposal. In particular, the concept of the benefiting area used in FEMA's BRIC program served as the foundation for Step 2 of our framework (see Chapter 3). In the next chapter, we draw on the strengths of these approaches to present a framework that is tailored to inform DAF infrastructure resilience decisionmaking.

---

[60] For more information on how the benefiting area concept is used in eligibility criteria for project scoping and mitigation projects, see FEMA, *Department of Homeland Security Notice of Funding Opportunity Fiscal Year 2021 Flood Mitigation Assistance*, 2021b. For additional details on how to develop the relevant project-level geospatial information, see FEMA, "New Geospatial File Eligibility Criteria in Flood Mitigation Grant Applications," June 2020.

[61] For additional analysis, see Noreen Clancy, Melissa L. Finucane, Jordan R. Fischbach, David G. Groves, Debra Knopman, Karishma V. Patel, and Lloyd Dixon, *The Building Resilient Infrastructure and Communities Mitigation Grant Program: Incorporating Hazard Risk and Social Equity into Decisionmaking Processes*, Homeland Security Operational Analysis Center operated by the RAND Corporation, RR-A1258-1, 2022.

[62] FEMA, *Department of Homeland Security Notice of Funding Opportunity Fiscal Year 2021 Building Resilient Infrastructure and Communities*, 2021a.

Chapter 3. A Framework for Prioritizing Resilience Projects

Resilience projects may take many forms—ranging from those that are explicitly identified as such to those that that may have incidental resilience benefits that might not otherwise be identified via other processes. *Projects* in this context may be (1) retrofits or improvements to existing assets that raise the hazard resilience of those assets, (2) new assets that raise the resilience of other assets at the installation, or (3) new assets intended to replace older assets whose baseline resilience standard is higher than the assets they replace. Each project provides benefits in unique ways across distinct geographic areas—yet is connected to other functions, systems, and missions, impacts to which must also be considered when assessing a project's value. Therefore, the framework described in this chapter facilitates the direct comparison of projects with an *explicit* or *implicit* climate resilience focus by enumerating (and, where possible, quantifying) their potential benefits as measured by multiple metrics.

The framework consists of four steps briefly summarized below and described in detail in the following sections. Implementing the framework requires that certain datasets first be obtained and preprocessed to serve as metrics in later steps in the framework. Step 0 must be performed for any installation at which projects will be evaluated but does not need to be repeated for evaluating additional projects at the same installation. Following Step 0, each step draws on one or more steps of the adapted RDVM framework described in Chapter 2. The steps of the framework are as follows:

- **Step 0—Build datasets to support resilience-based decisionmaking:** Describe the data and outline the data preprocessing steps required to prepare asset-level and unit-level metrics for evaluating the resilience benefits of installation projects.
- **Step 1—Characterize asset exposure:** Describe the level of hazard exposure (demonstrated here for flood and wildfire) that could occur at the installation(s) where a project is proposed as indicated by widely used geospatial hazard data, expressed in terms of the asset-level and unit-level metrics formulated in Step 0. This step is analogous to adapted RDVM Steps 3 and 4 and precedes the adapted RDVM Steps 1 and 2 to inform our selection of the installations serving as illustrative case studies for our framework.
- **Step 2—Identify the project's benefiting area:** Identify the specific assets at the installation that benefit from the enhanced resilience afforded by the project, determined by the properties of the project itself and the site-specific context in which it would be implemented. This step is analogous to adapted RDVM Steps 1 and 2 and directly informed by the benefiting area concept used in FEMA's BRIC program (see Chapter 2).
- **Step 3—Describe the project's exposure reduction potential:** Quantify the degree to which the proposed project, if implemented, would reduce exposure to the hazard(s) of interest, expressed in terms of the asset-level and unit-level metrics formulated in Step 0. This step is analogous to adapted RDVM Steps 5 and 6.

- **Step 4—Compare projects based on potential resilience benefits:** Informed by the results of Step 3 and the decisionmaker's own judgment, prioritize projects based on their relative resilience benefits in the context of mission objectives, broader goals in the DAF enterprise, and climate uncertainty. This step has no direct analog with RDVM but depends on outputs analogous to those obtained from adapted RDVM Step 6.

Step 0—Build Datasets to Support Resilience-Based Decisionmaking

To assess potential resilience benefits of projects, our framework uses data from across the DAF enterprise and from publicly available sources. These datasets, either individually or in combination with other datasets, provide metrics that can be used to illustrate infrastructure and mission exposure to climate hazards. Although not all metrics might be of equal interest to all users of the proposed framework, we sought to incorporate as many metrics as were available or able to be generated with relative ease. In this section, we describe the data preprocessing steps necessary to obtain metrics for analysis in Steps 1 and 3 of the framework, under the following two categories:

- **Assets:** number, percentage, and plant replacement value (PRV) of (1) total assets at an installation and (2) critical assets with high Tactical Mission Dependency Index (TMDI) values and high values of the constituent parts of TMDI (interruptibility and replicability) by generalized squadron type.[63] Data sources include TMDI provided by AFIMSC and asset locations and attributes from GeoBase, Real Property Asset Database (RPAD), and DAF facility standards.
- **Units:** number of unit types at an installation with low *slack* (see the "Unit-Level Metrics" section), determined by (1) the *uniqueness* of the unit type (i.e., the number of other installations that have the same unit type) and (2) the degree of exposure risk to the same hazard at the same time of year. Data sources include locations of missions from Defense Readiness Reporting System –Strategic (DRRS-S); relative hazard exposure risk from SWP worksheets; and hazard seasonality from the U.S. Geological Survey (USGS) and U.S. Forest Service.

Asset-Level Metrics

To represent installation assets and their associated attributes in our framework, we identified datasets that satisfied three conditions: (1) wide availability within the DAF to enable broad utilization of the framework; (2) spatial resolution at the scale of individual buildings; and (3)

---

[63] Our decision may embed other assumptions associated with the metrics. For example, PRV (a metric for quantifying the current value of a facility, determined from the cost to build a similar facility with the same production capability) is highly correlated with square footage—biasing the metric toward larger buildings but not necessarily ones that might generate a high amount of mission outputs per unit area—and does not include the high-value equipment contained in the facility (e.g., flight simulators). These limitations of PRV could be overcome by augmenting it with data on the value of equipment or other indicators of the asset value.

TMDI serves as a proxy for the relative importance of assets to mission. However, TMDI might soon be phased out in favor of other measures of the mission-relevance of assets, but we use it here as a stand-in given it is available for installations across the enterprise.

spatial coverage across the enterprise to enable comparisons between projects at multiple installations. Three key datasets satisfy these conditions: AFCEC's GeoBase installation facility database, AFIMSC's TMDI dataset, and the Office of the Assistant Secretary of Defense Sustainment's RPAD. These datasets can also be cross-referenced using each asset's Real Property Unique Identifier (RPUID). In addition, squadrons, tenants, and unit types associated with assets can be linked to other systems, such as the DRRS-S, to characterize exposure not just to assets but also to the functions and missions they support (see "Unit-Level Metrics" section below).[64]

For hazard exposure analysis (Step 1), we defined *assets* as buildings represented in GeoBase with a polygonal footprint to compute geospatial intersections with floodplain extents and burn probability maps. (Point-based assets, such as a control tower with undescribed dimensions, and linear assets, such as a utility conduit that may be drawn or configured differently between installations, were excluded.) Similarly, we excluded large-area features, such as runways and hardstands, as how these assets are segmented could have a disproportionate impact on the number of assets exposed. The DAF might choose to include additional asset types in its analysis of hazard exposure beyond those we use to illustrate the framework in this report.

Steps 1 and 3 of our framework generally aggregate the metrics listed above at the squadron level. We use *generalized squadron type* to refer to collapsed categories of squadrons at a given installation (e.g., at Seymour Johnson AFB, we group the 4th Aircraft Maintenance Squadron [AMXS], Component Maintenance Squadron, Equipment Maintenance Squadron, and Maintenance Group [MXG], hereafter referred to as *maintenance*) to provide a high-level view of exposed mission functions at the installation and to prevent inadvertent identification of specific installations in this report (e.g., it might be easy to identify certain installations with highly specialized squadrons or unique mixes of squadron types if the names of those squadrons were included). The TMDI dataset identifies a squadron owner for every asset with a RPUID attribute in GeoBase (collapsed into the full list of generalized squadron types provided in Appendix C), which also explains our approach to generating the squadron types.[65]

---

[64] We characterized asset exposure by unit (typically but not always squadrons) rather than by Category Code (CATCODE)—a numerical identifier assigned based on the functions of the facility—for two reasons. First, units provide a more accurate mapping of assets to mission functions than do CATCODEs, acknowledging that two assets with the same CATCODE might support two different missions. Second, given TMDI provides just one measure of the mission relevance of assets, we wanted to explore other ways to tie asset and installation exposure to mission impacts, and at least one relevant data source (DRRS-S) uses units and unit types as its organizing construct. Our prior experience with DRRS-S data pointed to the dataset's potential usefulness for differentiating among units based on the uniqueness of the tasks that they perform and, in turn, the mission impacts that might result from their exposure to hazards.

[65] Assets from the TMDI data are occasionally listed under the same RPUID, occasionally with different TMDI scores. We attribute this to multiple squadrons or tenants, with varying degrees of mission impact, occupying the same space, for instance, by sharing office space in the same building. In such cases, we assume the highest TMDI score for the RPUID.

As indicated above, we also considered other asset attributes, such as asset age, in characterizing exposure and ultimately in estimating a project's exposure reduction potential. Assets that are equally exposed to a particular hazard might not be equally affected by that hazard, owing in part to different design standards in place at the time of their construction. To explore the influence of design standards on potential impact to assets, we reviewed DAF UFC and AFI documents for engineering standards relevant to wildfire and flood risks.[66] The standards reviewed apply to both new and existing construction and concern risk characterization, as well as siting and construction guidelines in the presence of identified risk. After identifying these standards, we compiled a document history to construct timelines detailing the development of present standards. We used these timelines to approximate the engineered resilience of both installations and buildings within installations. Full results from this review are presented in the "Review of Facilities Standards" section of Appendix A.

Matching the facility built year attribute in GeoBase to the standards in place at the time of construction, we find that standards for infrastructure at DAF installations can be grouped into three distinct construction eras relevant to flood (1977 and prior, 1977–2002, and 2002 and later) and wildfire (2006 and prior, 2006–2016, and 2016 and later). Analysis of construction eras across the enterprise reveals that many DAF assets were built before 1977, when Executive Order (EO) 11988 established foundational flood engineering standards.[67] Furthermore, construction standards specific to wildfire did not exist until 2006.[68] The "Facilities Standards in Installation Case Studies" section in Appendix C provides further detail on the construction eras relevant to flood and wildfire for assets in GeoBase. We note that GeoBase does not provide information on whether assets were built to more-resilient standards than required at the time or whether the buildings have had mitigation measures put in place since their initial construction.

Construction era information provides only a limited understanding of the potential impact of exposure to an asset, as being built to an older standard does not necessarily mean that a particular asset is likely to sustain additional damage from exposure or that such damage may impair function to a higher degree. Likewise, an asset may have had its resilience improved (e.g., through hardening, retrofits, etc.) following its initial construction, which would not have been captured in its built year attribute. For these reasons, we include construction era information in a selected notional case study (Installation A, described below in Step 1) to illustrate how asset age and its associated construction standard(s) might be considered as a proxy for potential impact but do not explicitly consider how such information could be used to assess a project's exposure reduction (Step 3).

---

[66] A complete list and discussion of the UFC and AFI documents reviewed are provided in the "Organizational Comparison Documents" section of Appendix A.

[67] EO 11988, "Floodplain Management," Executive Office of the President, May 24, 1977.

[68] DoD, 2006.

We recognize that one of the goals of TMDI is to provide an assessment of the relative criticality of DAF assets. Although TMDI represents one important indicator of mission impact tied to unit assets, it is a relatively new metric that relies on operator self-assessment of asset replicability and interruptability, which may be inconsistent across the DAF enterprise. Furthermore, the assignment of a TMDI score to an asset might reflect only the asset's importance to a given installation (rather than to the enterprise as a whole), depending on the assessor's interpretation.[69]

Here, we augment TMDI with additional information that allows us to define a metric or set of metrics that characterize the *slack* in the enterprise system of installations: If one unit contributing to a DAF mission is damaged at a location, how many other locations have the same type of unit and could presumably carry out some or all of the affected unit's mission? Furthermore, in the context of natural hazards and climate change, how many of these locations could be potentially affected by the same hazard at approximately the same time of year? We characterize a unit supporting a given mission as having low slack if (1) the unit is relatively unique in that few other locations have the same unit type and (2) locations with the same unit type have similar hazard seasonality, indicating the potential for a single hazard event to affect units at both locations simultaneously.

In contrast to TMDI, which is assigned at the asset level, we characterize the slack for each unit type at an installation. We use the unit type assigned to each reporting unit in the DRRS-S system to illustrate the concept. Examples of these unit types include a Civil Engineering Squadron, operational units for a specific mission design series (MDS), and maintenance units for a specific MDS. These unit types are similar to the generalized squadron types discussed above; however, the DRRS-S unit types are more granular, particularly regarding the type of operations or maintenance unit, which are differentiated based on the specific weapon system they support. Given classification restrictions on the DRRS-S dataset, all results presented in this report that draw on that dataset are notional.

We mapped the generalized squadron types described above to DRRS-S unit types by using the specific unit names as the linking variable. Each specific unit was assigned both a generalized squadron type and a DRRS-S unit type. All assets in GeoBase for which we had TMDI information (and therefore the asset's tenant squadron) were used to determine the squadrons that would be mapped to unit types at a given installation. For each unit type, we identified all locations in which those unit types could be found. This list of locations serves as the primary basis for assessing the uniqueness of a given unit type. For instance, a unit type for which there is only one other location with the same unit type might be considered relatively unique (or a unit for which there is low slack in the enterprise system of units and installations to

---

[69] A4C personnel, conversation with authors, September 9, 2022.

handle any disruptions to its operation).[70] Similarly, a unit type with many locations might be considered less unique. It is worth noting that this analysis could be applied to resilience project prioritization beyond the context of natural hazards.

We apply this uniqueness analysis in the framework described below when considering the impact of exposure (and, conversely, resilience benefits) on units. For example, the uniqueness of units with exposed assets can serve as a metric for understanding the DAF enterprise-level effect of exposure to a particular hazard. Then, when estimating the reduction in exposure that a given project would yield, uniqueness could once again be used as a metric for characterizing the significance of units whose exposure is reduced by implementing the project in question. Table 3.1 presents an example of how uniqueness could be scaled, using the relevant number of unit locations, to determine differences in the uniqueness of exposed unit types, as shown in the notional results in Step 1.

Table 3.1. Notional Ranges for Unit Type Uniqueness Categories

Uniqueness	Number of Locations
High	1–2
Medium	3–10
Low	11+

In addition, unit slack is affected by whether it is likely that other installations that could replicate the function of assets at the impacted installation are exposed to the same hazard at approximately the same time of year. To illustrate this concept, we used responses to the SWP Appendix B worksheets, obtained from more than 100 DAF installations, to determine whether installations have high exposure to the same hazard at the same time of year.[71] Entries in the SWP Appendix B worksheets provide a first-order estimate of relative installation-level hazard exposure risk using a qualitative scale of low, medium, high, and extremely high.[72] We considered installations with a risk rating of medium or higher for a given hazard to be *at risk* to the hazard. Then, for each unit type, we counted the number of installations that have at least one

---

[70] This uniqueness definition treats all DAF functions as equal and necessary without a weighting on higher-priority missions.

[71] In 2020, AFCEC produced the SWP to provide a framework to screen and assess severe weather, climate hazards, and their current and future risks to DAF installations. SWP Appendix B serves as a screening worksheet for installation professionals to report their installation's susceptibility to severe weather and climate hazards and assess their relative risk. See Office of the Director of Civil Engineers, 2020.

[72] The data also provide risk ratings for high winds. For each hazard, there is also a risk rating for the current climate state. We chose to use the future rating to better consider the environment that a project must endure in its lifetime, however, the data would allow both to be incorporated.

unit of that type and are at risk to each of the two hazards in our analysis (flood and wildfire). Within the set of installations at risk for a hazard and with at least one unit of a specific unit type, we identified installations having a period of high hazard risk occurring during the same season, acknowledging that flood and wildfire risks have distinct seasonal cycles that vary by region. The table of DAF installations and their seasons of peak wildfire and flood risk, as well as the method for determining installation hazard seasonality, are provided in the "Installation Hazard Risk Seasonality" section of Appendix C.[73]

Step 1—Characterize Asset Exposure

To provide illustrative examples of how a project might offer resilience benefits, we created maps of plausible flood and wildfire exposure at four sample installations (see the "Hazard Exposure Methodology" section of Appendix C for a detailed methodology). To select the installations, we first obtained maps of the 1 percent annual exceedance probability (AEP) flood extent from the Defense Installations Spatial Data Infrastructure (DISDI), as used in DCAT, for 74 CONUS and outside the CONUS (OCONUS) active component main installation areas (i.e., not ranges or outlying sites).[74] We then spatially intersected GeoBase buildings with these flood extents in a geographic information system to determine the number and characteristics of assets exposed. We then selected 15 installations with the highest percentage of either building number or PRV exposed to flood relative to all assets at the installation, and further down-selected ten installations with the greatest number of high-TMDI assets by either exposed absolute building number or PRV.[75] Of these, we chose three notionally representative flood case study installations (A, B, and C) to span the installations that varied across both high numbers of exposed assets and high exposed PRV. We then identified two of these installations (A and B) as also having high wildfire exposure from DCAT documentation and DoD and DAF assessments. As Installation C does not have elevated wildfire exposure, we selected Installation D, which has a similar mission profile to Installation C, to represent a third case study for wildfire. A list of all installations considered for case studies is given in the "Hazard Exposure Methodology" section of Appendix C.

From the fire and flood exposure maps, we estimated the number of exposed GeoBase assets (and, for selected installations, the number of exposed assets in each construction era) and the percentage of the total assets belonging to each generalized squadron type that is exposed. We

---

[73] Because of data limitations from the flood and wildfire data, this table is limited to installations on CONUS. For locations OCONUS, this filter would be omitted or require additional information on the seasonal hazard risk.

[74] Current flood extents for installation boundaries in DCAT are based on historical data obtained from the FEMA National Flood Hazard Layer for the 1 percent AEP event or 2D hydrologic and hydraulic modeling on a 10-meter digital elevation model where FEMA data are lacking (Pinson et al., 2021).

[75] In conversation with the sponsor, we consider TMDI >=80 to be of highest concern for project prioritization in this report, but this threshold can be changed per the preferences of the framework user.

then used TMDI to identify the assets that would cause the greatest disruption to operations if they were to fail because of low interruptability and/or replicability. We also analyzed exposed assets by the constituent parts of their TMDI score as follows:

- Interruptability—How fast would the response action be if the real property asset's operations were interrupted?
- Replicability—How difficult would it be to relocate or replicate the mission-enabling capabilities of the real property asset if they were interrupted?[76]
- Our exposure analysis included assets with either *immediate* (<15 minutes) or *brief* (<24 hours) interruptability, as well as assets that are either impossible or extremely difficult to replicate. For example, Table 3.2 shows these values for a flood exposure scenario by generalized squadron type at Installation A, where

  - 70 percent of the operations squadron type's assets are exposed to flood, of which 64 percent are rated as having high TMDI (>=80)
  - only two communications' squadron type assets are exposed to flood; however, these constitute of one-half of their total assets.

As described above, we also assessed the relative uniqueness of unit types affected at the installation as a proxy for the function each unit provides as part of a DAF enterprise mission. We show this metric for Installation A only as it is notional at this level of classification.

Flood Exposure Analysis

Tables 3.2 and 3.3 demonstrate the variability in the scale of flood exposure at two notional installations (A and C). At Installation A, the operations squadron type is the most exposed by the number of exposed assets, percentage of assets exposed, and the total PRV exposed, and it has the greatest number of exposed assets in the earliest construction era (pre-1977). The high number of assets built before 1977 indicates that much of the operations squadron type's asset portfolio originated before the establishment of modern flood engineering criteria, such as the requirement that structures within floodplains must, if practicable, be elevated above the flood level associated with the 1 percent AEP (see the "Review of Facilities Standards" section in Appendix A). In addition, many of these assets have high TMDI, with the units they support being highly unique. Other squadron types that support operations, such as maintenance or logistics and readiness, are somewhat less exposed, although they still have high mission dependency and variable uniqueness. Construction era information and uniqueness values are shown for Installation A (Table 3.2) to illustrate the potential value of such information for exposure analysis but are omitted from later tables for ease of interpretation.

---

[76] Russell Weniger, "Setting Priorities: Tactical MDI Aligns Facilities to Mission," *Air Force Civil Engineer*, Vol. 26, No. 1, 2018.

Table 3.2. Installation A Baseline Exposure Analysis Based on DCAT 1 Percent AEP Riverine Flood

Generalized Squadron Type	Number of Exposed Assets (Pre-'77, '77–'02, Post-'02)	Percentage of Assets Exposed	PRV Exposed (Pre-'77, '77–'02, Post-'02)	TMDI			Unit Type Uniqueness (Notional)
				Number of Exposed Assets >=80	Number of Exposed Assets with > Brief Interruptability	Number of Exposed Assets with > Extremely Difficult Replicability	
C2, Administration, and Management	2 (0,1,1)	9	$7.9M (0,4.2,3.7)	—	—	—	M
Communications Support	2 (1,0,1)	20	$11.9M (6.0,0,5.9)	1	1	1	L
Engineering Support	7 (3,2,2)	11	$32.8M (4.9,22.3,5.5)	1	1	2	L
Force Support	21 (6,10,3)	32	$119.6M (42.1,61.1,30.9)	1	6	6	L
Logistics and Readiness	13 (7,5,1)	38	$33.6M (30.0,2.2,1.4)	5	5	10	L
Maintenance	19 (9,8,2)	33	$94.1M (71.1,22.5,5.0)	5	6	6	H
Medical Services	2 (0,2,0)	40	$93.2M (0,93.1,0)	—	—	—	L
Operations	31 (15,11,5)	82	$373.1M (173.0,181.9,18.3)	20	21	19	H
Operations Support	3 (2,0,1)	6	$26.9M (19.2,0,7.7)	2	2	3	M
Reserves and Guard	1 (0,1,0)	100	$3.5M (0,3.5,0)	—	—	—	L
Security Forces	3 (0,2,1)	11	$3.6M (0,2.3,1.3)	—	—	—	L
Tenant	1 (1,0,0)	100	$5.1M (5.1,0,0)	—	—	—	N/A
Training and Range	2 (1,1,0)	11	$23.8M (17.3,6.5,0)	—	—	—	M
Total	103 (45,41,17)	27	$755.1M (368.7,306.6,79.8)	36	43	49	N/A

SOURCE: Features information from DCAT, RPAD, GeoBase, TMDI, RAND geospatial analysis, and RAND analysis of DRRS-S data.

NOTE: C2 = command and control; H = high; L = low; M = medium ; N/A = not applicable. Dashes indicate where no assets were exposed.

In contrast, Installation C has 21 more total assets exposed than Installation A, representing only 10 percent more of the total assets on the installation but nearly double the PRV exposure (Table 3.3). At least one-quarter of all assets are at risk for all exposed squadron types, suggesting the potential for extensive disruption to operations. Flood exposure analysis for another notional installation (Installation B) is included in the "Additional Baseline Hazard Exposure Results" section of Appendix C to show additional potential variation.

Table 3.3. Installation C Baseline Exposure Analysis Based on DCAT 1 Percent AEP Riverine Flood

Generalized Squadron Type	Number of Exposed Assets	Percentage of Assets Exposed	PRV Exposed	TMDI		
				Number of Exposed Assets >=80	Number of Exposed Assets with > Brief Interruptability	Number of Exposed Assets with > Extremely Difficult Replicability
C2, Administration, and Management	11	48	$567.7M	7	7	7
Communications Support	7	58	$312.3M	4	4	4
Engineering Support	28	46	$125.6M	2	2	5
Force Support	27	24	$175.9M	—	2	—
Logistics and Readiness	16	48	$51.3M	4	5	6
Maintenance	4	57	$94.1M	2	2	2
Medical Services	4	29	$24.0M	—	—	—
Operations	8	89	$115.9M	1	1	1
Operations Support	6	26	$83.1M	3	3	3
Other	1	50	$0.3M	—	—	—
Security Forces	2	50	$23.9M	1	1	—
Weather	9	43	$20.7M	3	3	4
Total	124	38	$1,626.5M	28	31	33

SOURCE: Features information from DCAT, RPAD, GeoBase, TMDI, and RAND geospatial analysis.

Wildfire Exposure Analysis

A similar baseline exposure analysis can be conducted using different exposure threshold metrics for wildfire, revealing patterns unique to that hazard (Table 3.4; see the "Hazard

Exposure Methodology" section of Appendix C for detailed methodology). For example, Installation B is large and required merging together multiple FlamMap landscape input files and multiple model runs to generate sufficient areal coverage and density of simulated fire ignitions.[77] In Table 3.4, we show that disproportionate impact from exposure may be borne by the intelligence and reconnaissance squadron type (especially for low-interruptability assets); the operations squadron type (especially for low-replicability assets); and the C2, administration, and management squadron type (for both low-interruptability and low-replicability assets).

Table 3.4. Installation B Baseline Assets at Risk of Wildfire Exposure

Generalized Squadron Type	Number of Exposed Assets	Percentage of Assets Exposed	PRV Exposed	TMDI		
				Number of Exposed Assets >=80	Number of Exposed Assets with > Brief Interruptability	Number of Exposed Assets with > Extremely Difficult Replicability
C2, Administration, and Management	8	7	$15.8M	7	7	8
Engineering Support	22	8	$11.6M	2	2	2
Force Support	4	3	$3.0M	—	—	—
Intelligence and Reconnaissance	31	26	$35.2M	4	19	5
Logistics and Readiness	1	2	$2.4M	—	—	—
Maintenance	6	4	$7.9M	1	2	2
Operations	41	25	$148.0M	3	3	9
Operations Support	6	8	$49.4M	3	4	3
Other	3	2	$1.7M	—	—	2
Research and Testing	2	7	$0.2M	—	—	—
Security Forces	3	14	$3.3M	—	—	—
Space Force	1	7	$74.6M	1	1	1
Training and Range	15	8	$27.9M	—	3	—
Total	128	10	$381.0M	21	41	32

---

[77] FlamMap is a publicly available tool developed by the U.S. Forest Service to support a variety of fire and land management objectives. For more details, see the "Hazard Exposure Methodology" section of Appendix C.

Generalized Squadron Type	Number of Exposed Assets	Percentage of Assets Exposed	PRV Exposed	Number of Exposed Assets >=80	TMDI Number of Exposed Assets with > Brief Interruptability	Number of Exposed Assets with > Extremely Difficult Replicability

SOURCE: RPAD, GeoBase, TMDI, FlamMap, LANDFIRE, and RAND geospatial analysis.
NOTE: Because of the size of the installation and processing time constraints, we merged multiple lower-resolution FlamMap outputs and proportionately reduced the ignition probability threshold. The numbers and percentages likely represent a slight underestimate based on a cross-check with the full-resolution model for the intervention project area presented later in this chapter.

This analysis can be customized to include the effect of suppression resources. For example, Installation A adapts the typical analysis to screen for assets beyond a 1,000-meter response radius from existing fire stations.[78] Table 3.5 shows that 14 percent of operations squadron type's assets are exposed to wildfire risk in this scenario, of which one-half are rated as having high TMDI (>=80), whereas only 18 percent of operations support squadron type's assets are exposed to wildfire risk, but these comprise two-thirds of the total exposed PRV. Wildfire exposure analysis for another notional installation (Installation D) is included in the "Additional Baseline Hazard Exposure Results" section of Appendix C to show additional potential variation.

Table 3.5. Installation A Baseline Assets at Risk of Wildfire Exposure Outside a 1,000-Meter Response Radius from a Fire Station

Generalized Squadron Type	Number of Exposed Assets	Percentage of Assets Exposed	PRV Exposed	Number of Exposed Assets >=80	TMDI Number of Exposed Assets with > Brief Interruptability	Number of Exposed Assets with > Extremely Difficult Replicability	(Notional) Unit Type Uniqueness Considering Wildfire Risk
Force Support	5	9	$3.3M	—	—	—	L
Logistics and Readiness	8	10	$11.4M	—	1	2	L
Maintenance	8	14	$16.2M	1	1	1	H
Operations	6	14	$46.3M	3	3	2	H
Operations Support	9	18	$169.8M	6	6	4	M

---

[78] While previous research suggests that an average fire engine response speed of 35 miles per hour (Peter Kolesar, *A Model for Predicting Average Fire Company Travel Times*, RAND Corporation, R-1624-NYC, 1975), combined with National Fire Protection Agency (NFPA) standards calling for a 240-second first-engine response time (NFPA, "National Fire Codes Online," homepage, undated) would result in a slightly wider radius, we assumed a 1,000-meter response radius to account for slower response times over unpaved wildland terrain and obstacles common on the base peripheries.

| Generalized Squadron Type | Number of Exposed Assets | Percentage of Assets Exposed | PRV Exposed | TMDI | | | (Notional) Unit Type Uniqueness Considering Wildfire Risk |
				Number of Exposed Assets >=80	Number of Exposed Assets with > Brief Interruptability	Number of Exposed Assets with > Extremely Difficult Replicability	
Other	1	6	$0.3M	—	—	—	N/A
Security Forces	7	25	$12.5M	—	1	1	L
Total	41	10	$257.5M	10	11	10	N/A

SOURCE: RPAD, GeoBase, TMDI, FlamMap, LANDFIRE, RAND geospatial analysis, and RAND analysis of DRSS-S data.
NOTE: There was only one exposed asset of low mission dependency built after 2006 (security forces squadron type) and no exposed assets built in 2016 or later. H = high; L = low; M = medium; N/A = not applicable.

Step 2—Identify the Project's Benefiting Area

The benefiting area of a project—a concept used in FEMA's BRIC program and informed by a conception of resilience as an ability to withstand or avoid exposure (see Chapter 2)—may vary widely depending on a project's characteristics. It describes the area that would benefit from additional hazard resilience if a proposed project were to be implemented, and in so doing, it identifies the specific assets within that area that stand to benefit from the project. It is instrumental in defining the project's scope, which may vary from a single asset to potentially every asset at the installation.

To develop a method for identifying the benefiting area of projects, we first reviewed a list of MILCON projects under consideration for funding, several of which appeared to have some infrastructural or energy resilience benefits. Some of these projects would reduce hazard exposure by relocating or consolidating assets out of the floodplain, procuring and planning for the installation of temporary flood barriers, or building improved stormwater conveyance to reduce the extent of the floodplain. Other projects might also reduce the impact of hazard exposure by increasing redundancy and introducing excess capacity (e.g., an auxiliary fire station) or by allowing for greater self-sufficiency via islanding during an electrical outage.

Our review of MILCON projects revealed three main categories of projects. We use several notional case studies across four installations to illustrate how the benefiting area might be identified for each of the following project types:

- **structural** projects that create new assets or alter the characteristics of existing ones to remove people and property from hazard exposure through such activities as flood-proofing; fire suppression; or elevating, hardening, or relocating assets
- **interventional** projects that reduce the exposure of assets to a hazard, typically by creating a barrier (e.g., a firebreak or floodwall) that must be installed and maintained

31

- **landscape** projects that seek to alter the source of the hazard and limit its exposure (e.g., by altering the landscape to improve the conveyance of floodwaters), prevent the establishment of (wildfire) fuels, or provide defendable fire breaks.

The benefiting area for structural projects is limited to those assets that are specifically targeted by the project. For example, a structural project that relocates and consolidates assets out of the floodplain would include only impacts to those buildings. Therefore, the benefiting area for this class of projects is relatively easy to define. The benefiting area for interventional projects can be harder to define and requires estimating the effect that the project will have on assets that it serves to geographically separate from the hazard. Last, landscape-based projects may have a very large benefiting area because of their typical effect of reconstructing entire landscapes. In the case of flood, they may be specifically designed to reduce the area of the floodplain or the flood depth within the floodplain. Other projects such as stormwater or fuels management via green infrastructure and ecological best practices may require expert estimation. These project types and installation-based case studies are summarized in Table 3.6.

Table 3.6. Project Typologies and Notional Installation Projects

Installation	Structural		Interventional		Landscape	
	Fire	Flood	Fire	Flood	Fire	Flood
Installation A	Auxiliary fire station	Communications relocation	—	—	—	—
Installation B	—	—	Perimeter road with buffer area	Deployable barriers	—	—
Installation C	—	—	—	—	—	Stormwater conveyance and green infrastructure
Installation D	—	—	—	—	Phased solar panel field	—

Notional Flood Mitigation Projects

Flood exposure can occur on installations across vastly different scales. For example, localized heavy rain might overwhelm stormwater conveyance systems as occurred in 2019 at Beale AFB.[79] In contrast, an installation might be exposed to a regional hazard with impacts ranging beyond the reach of DAF decision processes, such as the flooding of the Missouri River at Offutt AFB in the same year.[80] In both cases, a percentage area-based understanding of the hazard extent (or, conversely, the potential benefit of a mitigation project) would have likely been a poor indicator of the extent of mission disruption expected to result from the exposure. At

---

[79] Juliana Londono, "Two Years After a Flood, the 9th PSPTS Reopens," *Air Force News*, August 20, 2021.

[80] Stephen Losey, "After Massive Flood, Offutt Looks to Build a Better Base," *Air Force Times*, August 7, 2020.

Beale AFB, one of the few buildings affected had critical below-grade spaces and forced the relocation of those functions, which were necessary for mission continuity. In contrast, at Offutt AFB, some of the airfield was inundated, but flight operations could continue on a shortened runway, and although many buildings were flooded, only a few held strategic value over the long term. To illustrate the application of this framework across a variety of potential hazard impacts, we present notional benefiting areas at three scales of intervention—a few buildings, a cluster of buildings, and a subwatershed of the installation. These correspond to the three different types of flood projects—structural (building elevation, relocation, and flood-proofing), landscape (stormwater conveyance improvements), and interventional (deployable flood barriers).

Small-Scale Structural Project at Installation A: Communications Facility Relocation and Consolidation

Installation A is typical of many DAF facilities, wherein local waterways bisect parts of the base that may be subject to flash flooding. Rainfall-induced flooding may be exacerbated by channelization of surface drainage in built-up areas. One potential flood mitigation strategy would be to relocate critical assets farther away from the floodplain and/or to higher ground. For example, several communication facilities at lower elevations relative to the surrounding blocks of the campus might be exposed to pluvial flooding. These building assets have a PRV of $19.2 million, and based on similar MILCON project descriptions we reviewed, we might anticipate a consolidated building to have a cost of around $30 million (see Figure 3.1 for the notional project area).[81] This project might not be deemed an effective use of limited resources on cost merits alone but may compete more effectively in the DAF project selection process when accounting for its resilience benefits and potential to reduce mission impact. In addition, this project may offer other benefits, such as modernization of obsolete equipment or facilities.

---

[81] Though costing these projects was not within the scope of our research, we included first-order estimates based on similar projects or unitized reference numbers for scale context and a preliminary comparison with the descriptive statistics of our benefiting area calculations.

Figure 3.1. Installation A Relocation and Consolidation Project

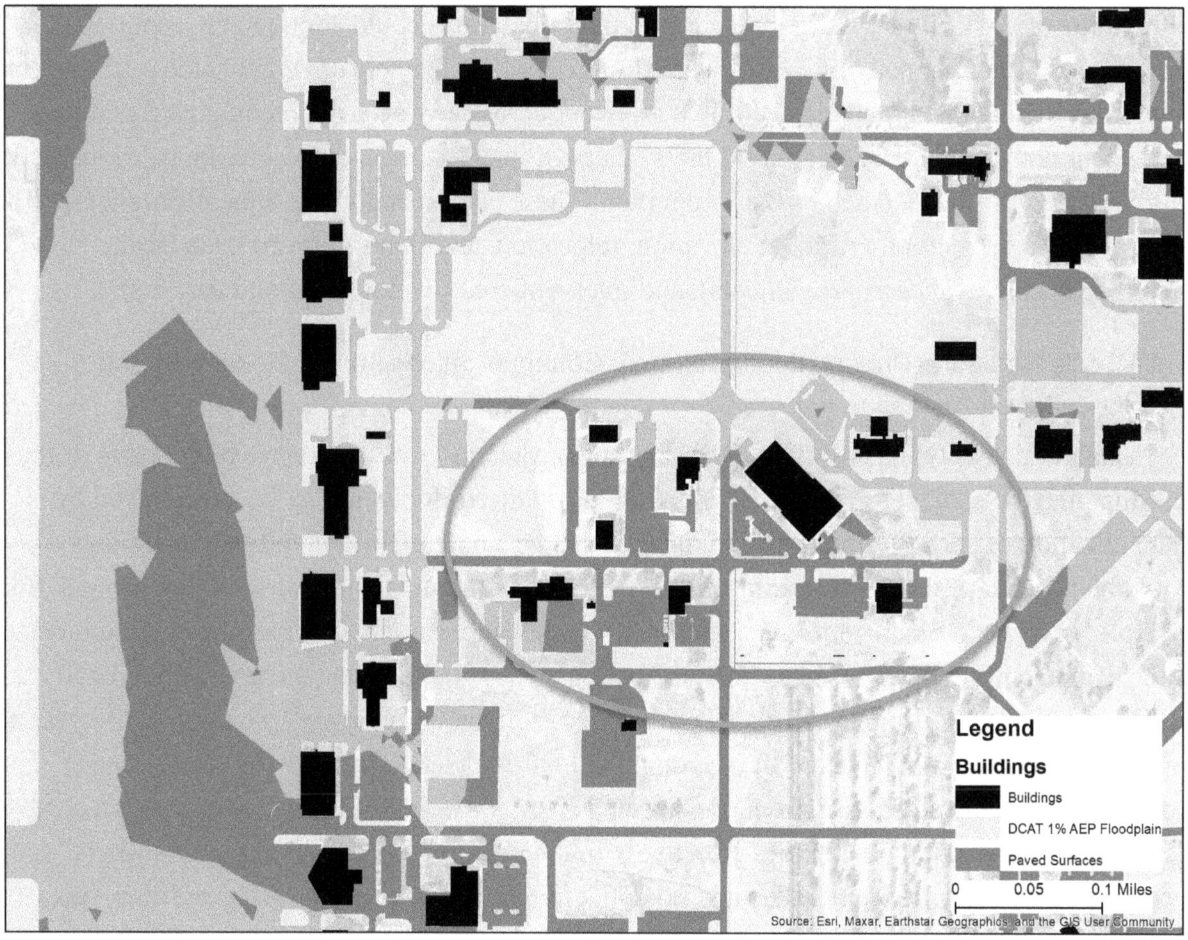

SOURCES: Map features Maxar imagery from 2020, created using ArcGIS software by Esri. Overlay data are from DCAT, GeoBase, and RAND geospatial analysis.

Medium-Scale Intervention at Installation B: Deployable Flood Barrier

A second example looks at another flooding phenomenon common to DAF installations—localized ponding around airfield assets because of their extensive impervious area. Hangars and other large industrial-scale facilities may have unique exposure patterns because of low sills and large openings to facilitate the movement of planes and other equipment. One strategy to protect these assets is to use deployable floodwalls to temporarily seal entrances or create defensible perimeters (Figure 3.2), which typically range in cost from approximately $400 per foot to $10 million per mile.[82] At Installation B, we consider approximately 5,000 feet of these barriers within the highlighted area in Figure 3.3, which would also include eight generators and 29

---

[82] For examples, see AquaFence, "Flood Wall," webpage, undated; and Flood Control International, "Flood Barriers," webpage, undated.

transformer pads. Such a project might also include a storage area for the panels, equipment to move them around the installation, and backup pumps in the event of seepage or a leak.

Figure 3.2. Example of a Deployable Flood Barrier Tested by North Dakota Air National Guard

SOURCE: Amy Wieser-Willson, "FLOOD NEWS: Guardsmen Install Flood Barrier Never Before Used in Fargo," *Air Force News*, March 17, 2010. Photo by David Lipp. For this, and similar subsequent images, the appearance of U.S. Department of Defense (DoD) visual information does not imply or constitute DoD endorsement.

Figure 3.3. Installation B Airfield Deployable Flood Barriers Project

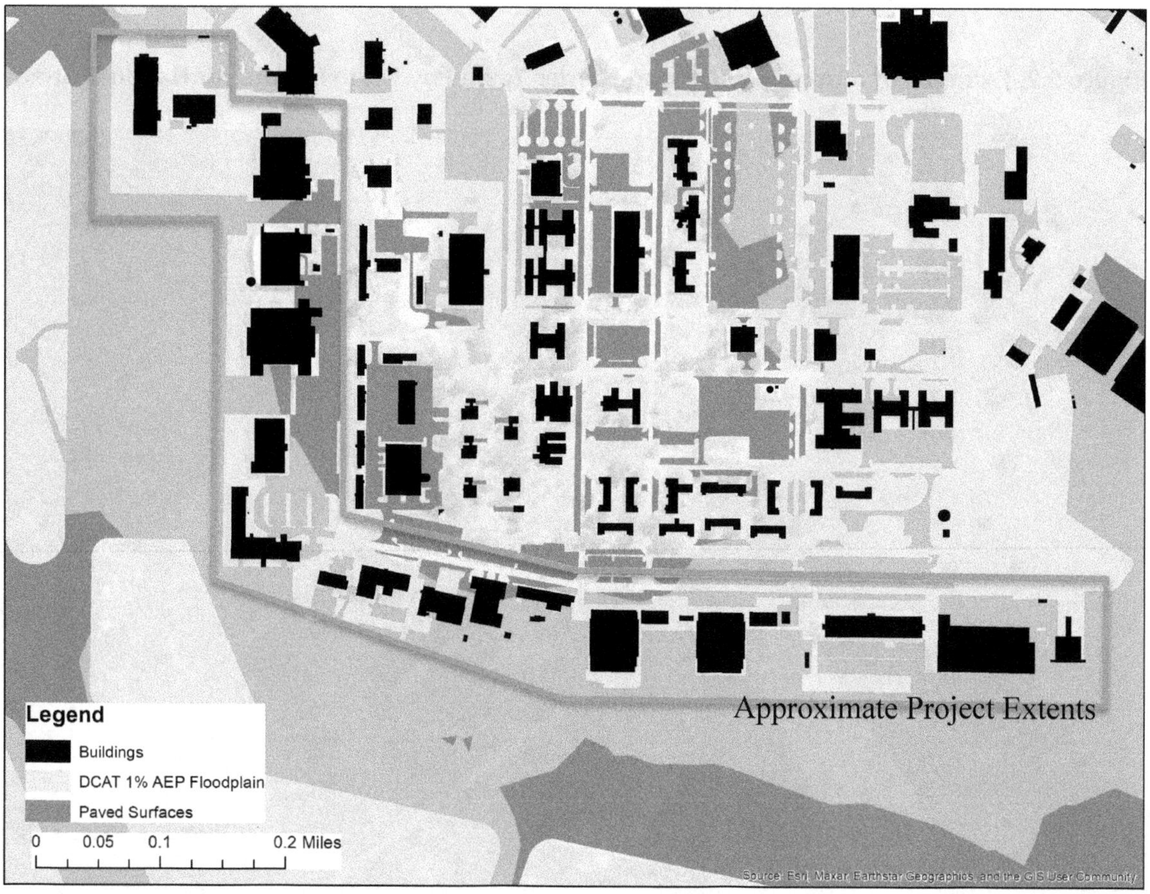

SOURCES: Map features Maxar imagery from 2020, created using ArcGIS software by Esri. Overlay data are from DCAT, GeoBase, and RAND geospatial analysis.

Large-Scale Landscape Project at Installation C: Green Infrastructure–Based Stormwater Conveyance Improvements

The final notional flood exposure project explores mitigation at the scale of the entire base or the surrounding area as part of a broader regional flood strategy. For example, Figure 3.4 shows one of a series of dams at Beale AFB that was recently removed to improve conveyance and local habitat. Installation C is in a flood-prone area with naturalized drainage systems that can easily be overwhelmed by seasonal heavy rain. Working in conjunction with the adjacent municipality, which is both upstream and downstream of the installation, base planners could outline a green infrastructure strategy that reduces flood exposure and augments the conveyance capacity of the creek by increasing the size of the culverts at several infrastructure crossings. Figure 3.5 shows a notional layout. As a rough order of magnitude for costs on the low end, a bottom-up estimate might suggest 14,000 feet of green infrastructure (approximately $5 million); 6,000 linear feet of naturalized revetment (approximately $4 million); and five culverts and associated improvements (approximately $10 million). Assuming one-half of the 350-acre area is impervious, these estimates suggest a total project cost up to $50 million.[83]

Figure 3.4. Example of Conveyance Improvement and Green Infrastructure Project at Beale AFB

SOURCE: Jennifer Schneider, "Air Force, USFWS Partner to Restore Fish Habitat," *Air Force News*, May 27, 2021. Photos by Alexandre Montes.

---

[83] Jordan R. Fischbach, Kyle Siler-Evans, Devin Tierney, Michael T. Wilson, Lauren M. Cook, and Linnea Warren May, *Robust Stormwater Management in the Pittsburgh Region: A Pilot Study*, RAND Corporation, RR-1673-MCF, 2017; Jordan R. Fischbach, Michael T. Wilson, Craig A. Bond, Ajay K. Kochhar, David Catt, and Devin Tierney, *Managing Heavy Rainfall with Green Infrastructure: An Evaluation in Pittsburgh's Negley Run Watershed*, RAND Corporation, RR-A564-1, 2020.

Figure 3.5. Installation C Stormwater Conveyance Improvement and Green Infrastructure Project

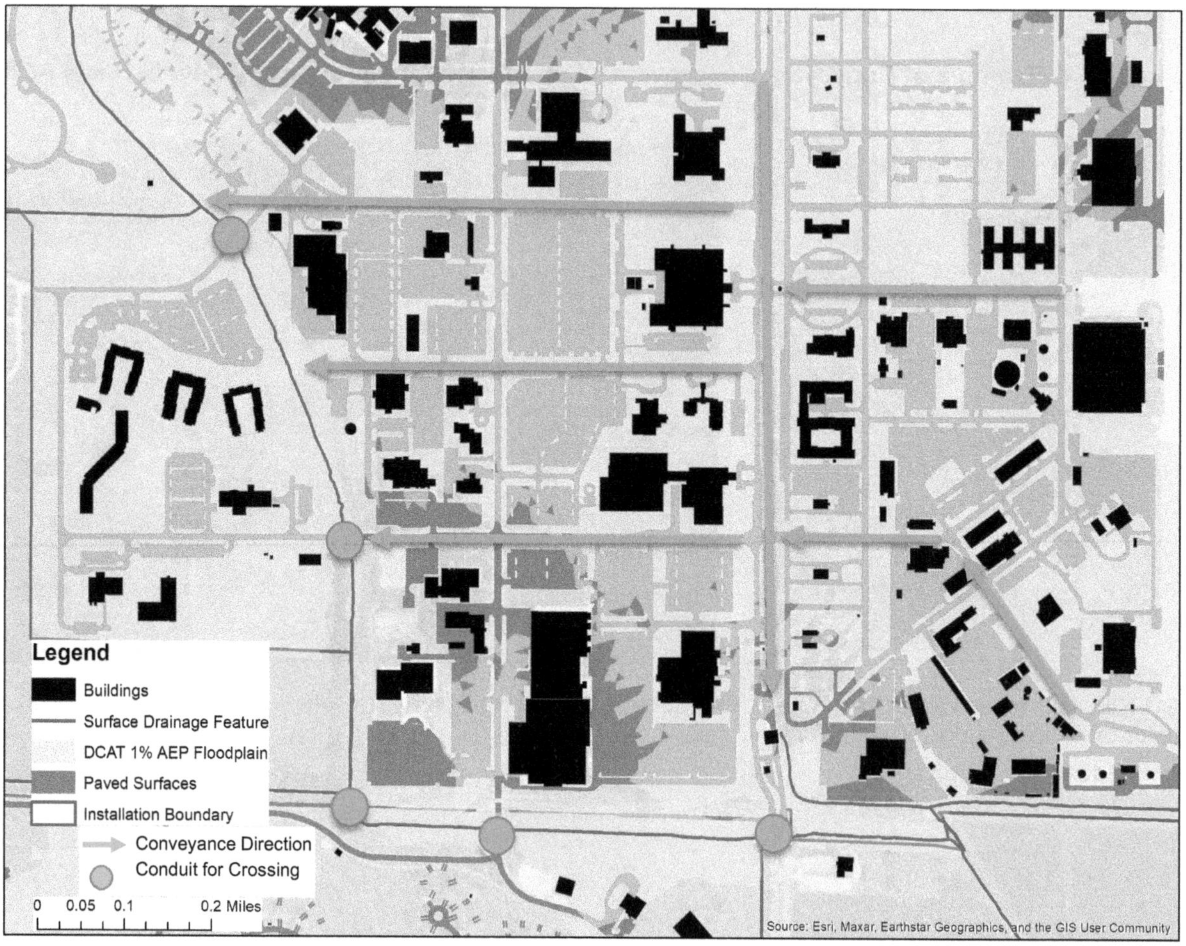

Legend
- Buildings
- Surface Drainage Feature
- DCAT 1% AEP Floodplain
- Paved Surfaces
- Installation Boundary
- Conveyance Direction
- Conduit for Crossing

0   0.05   0.1   0.2 Miles

Source: Esri, Maxar, Earthstar Geographics, and the GIS User Community

SOURCES: Map features Maxar imagery from 2022, created using ArcGIS software by Esri. Overlay data are from DCAT; Military Installations, Ranges, and Training Areas (MIRTA); GeoBase; and RAND geospatial analysis.
NOTE: Arrows indicate the flow patterns of the green stormwater infrastructure; dots show where larger conduits might be necessary to improve conveyance under road crossings, and other areas.

Notional Wildfire Mitigation Projects

The benefiting area assessment can also be conducted for wildfire mitigation projects. The following section follows a parallel structure to our flood analysis, starting with a small-scale notional structural project and ending with a large-scale notional landscape project.

Small-Scale Structural Project at Installation A: Auxiliary Fire Station

A key component of wildfire exposure management is the suppression provided by timely and capable response resources. DAF installations typically have fire stations associated with the airfield to respond to crashes and provide rescue, and, for those centrally located, to address structure fires and other incidents. Such facilities often provide wildland fire suppression and management functions, but elevated wildland fire exposure risk at some installations may require

38

additional dedicated response assets (e.g., hand crews, off-road capable fire engines, or specially equipped aerial assets) capable of fire suppression and management in the wildland or the wildland-urban interface (Figure 3.6).

Figure 3.6. Example of Auxiliary Equipment at Malmstrom AFB

SOURCE: Daniel Brosam, "Malmstrom AFB Receives New Fire Truck," *Air Force News*, July 12, 2017.

Installation A is one such place. Whereas a typical airfield fire station might have a PRV of $7 million, an auxiliary station with specialized wildland engines and equipment in an austere location might require additional infrastructural upgrades for water pressure and pumping, totaling approximately $20 million based on similar project descriptions. Figure 3.7 shows the baseline wildfire exposure from the FlamMap model and area covered by a proposed auxiliary fire station with a response radius of 1,000 meters. Assets falling within the service areas of the proposed project and existing fire stations are assumed to be protected from exposure in this analysis. We restrict the red-flag exposure assessment to buildings outside a 1,000-meter radius of an existing fire station as a notional proxy for where shorter response time or additional capabilities might be beneficial.[84]

Figure 3.7. Installation A Baseline Wildfire Exposure and Proposed Fire Station Service Area

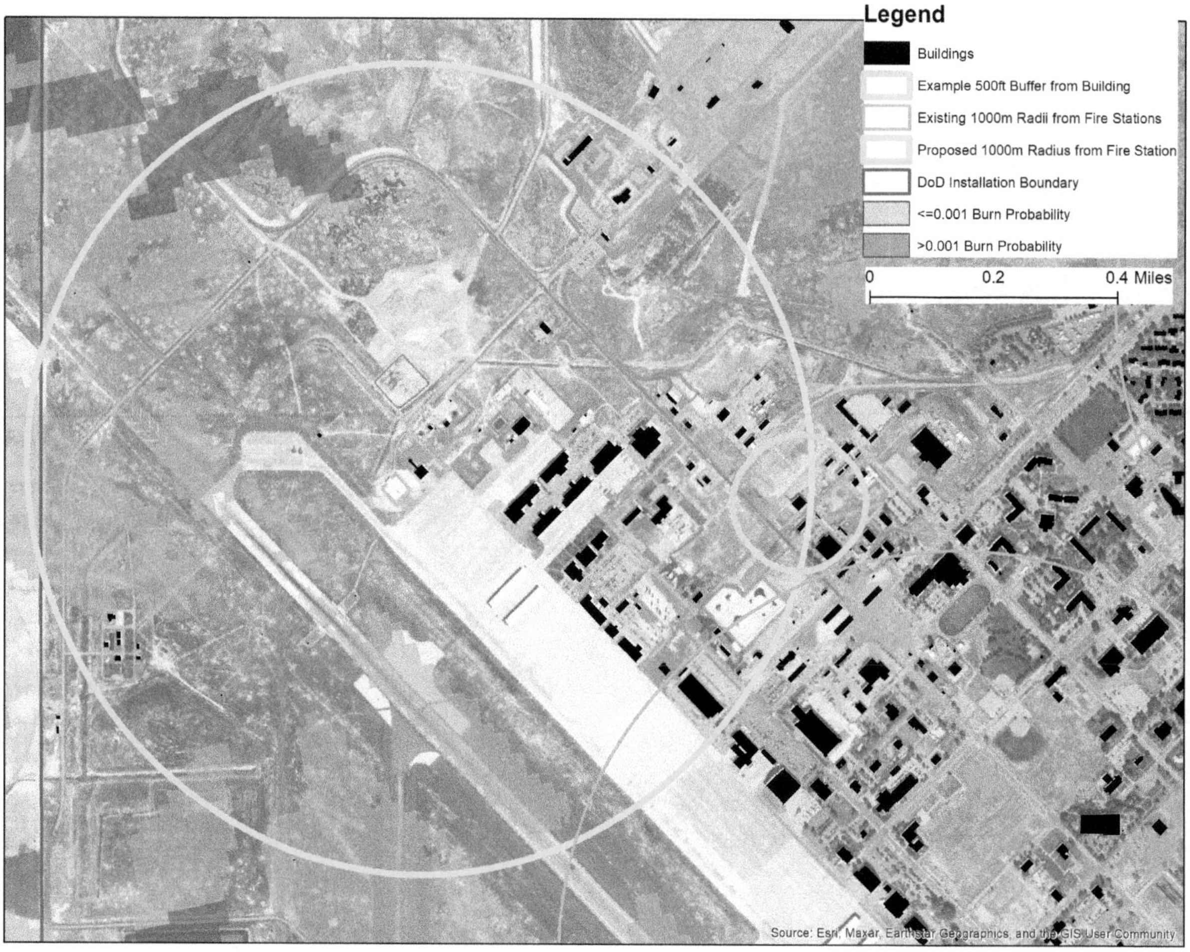

SOURCES: Map features Maxar imagery from 2021, created using ArcGIS software by Esri. Overlay data are from RPAD, GeoBase, TMDI, FlamMap, LANDFIRE, and RAND geospatial analysis.
NOTE: As this is a fire suppression project, we do not show postproject exposure risk from FlamMap.

Medium-Scale Intervention at Installation B: Security Improvements Along Perimeter Road

Whereas the above project at Installation A improves fire suppression within the benefiting area, the following project aims to reduce the potential extent of a wildfire burn area. We examine an austere facility that is in the process of upgrading its security by establishing a paved perimeter patrol road that will also serve as a fire break. The project will also clear an 800-foot-

---

[84] Red-flag warning conditions consist of locally defined parameters where higher temperatures, lower humidity levels, and stronger winds elevate the fire risk and certain types of activities are encouraged or enforced to be curtailed. This warning is an unrelated concept to RED FLAG aerial combat training exercises.

wide vegetation area around the perimeter to improve visibility and conduct site preparation for future potential expansion. The total cost is approximately $2.5 million per mile of new road and $2,500 per linear foot of security fencing for the resulting 3-mile perimeter and 340-acre cleared area.

By creating and maintaining a perimeter barrier clear of vegetation, the project not only reduces the potential for wildfire spread but also reduces the amount of fuel (i.e., the vegetation) available, resulting in a lower probability of ignition and reduced rates of fire spread. We note that climate change could exacerbate dry conditions at many installations, raising the importance of fuel management, a substantial challenge for the DAF going forward (Figure 3.8).[85] Fuel management efforts must also account for local seasonal conditions and smoke concerns of base personnel and neighboring residents.

Figure 3.8. Example of Fuels Management at Hurlburt Field

SOURCE: "Large-Scale Prescribed Burn Near Hurlburt Field Jan. 30," *Air Force News*, January 29, 2021. Photo by Samuel King, Jr.

Figure 3.9 shows that existing fire breaks (red lines) may appear to have a modest absolute impact on wildfire exposure as modeled by FlamMap. In part, this modest impact is because of

---

[85] Pinson et al., 2021.

the localized nature of that wildfire hazard and the fact that even regularly cleared land will still maintain a degree of flammability when light grasses and shrubs return between treatments. Such results are also a testament to existing mitigation protocols already in place by the DAF.

Figure 3.9. Installation B Baseline Wildfire Exposure with Intervention Area Shown

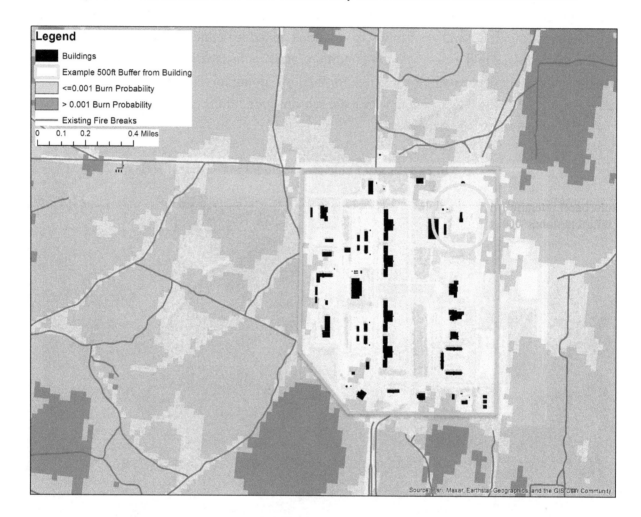

SOURCES: Map features Maxar imagery from 2022, created using ArcGIS software by Esri. Overlay data are from GeoBase, FlamMap, LANDFIRE, and RAND geospatial analysis.

Large-Scale Landscape Project at Installation D: Phased Solar Panel Farm

The DAF has made energy assurance an enterprise-level priority. To improve energy resilience, a decisionmaker may choose to augment an installation's generation capabilities within the fence line, provide microgrid-based islanding, reduce utility costs, and/or decrease dependency on carbon-based fuels. For example, Eglin AFB recently installed a 240-acre solar panel array (Figure 3.10). Although this type of project may have been proposed through a different planning process, this and similar projects might carry incidental wildfire resilience benefits because space around the project would likely be cleared and/or maintained differently, thereby reducing the burnable area on the base.

Figure 3.10. Example of 240-Acre Solar Array at Eglin AFB

SOURCE: Cheryl Sawyers, "First Panel Installed at Eglin's Solar Farm," *Air Force News*, January 20, 2017. Photo by Samuel King, Jr.

Our notional project considers two phases (145 acres [Phase 1] and 90 acres [Phase 2]) of a similar approximately $80 million solar panel array at Installation D that could produce on the order of 30–60MW of power. In addition, the figure shows the baseline wildfire exposure given the previously described red-flag conditions. Figures 3.11 and 3.12 show the estimated wildfire exposure (i.e., burn probability) before the completion either Phase 1 or 2, respectively.

Figure 3.11. Installation D Baseline Wildfire Exposure with Phase 1 of Solar Panel Project Outlined

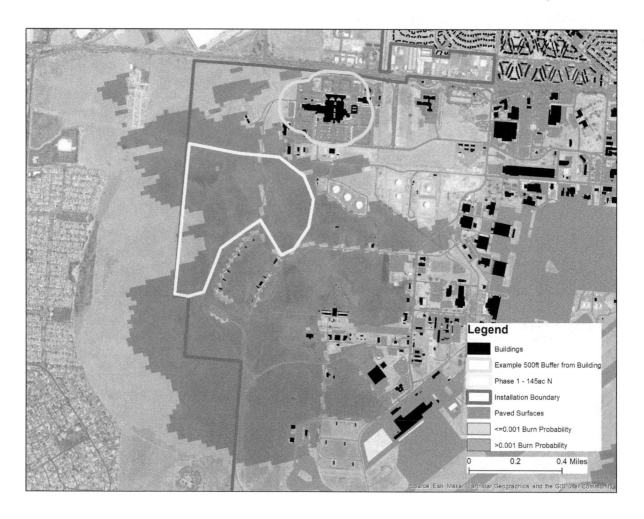

SOURCES: Map features Maxar imagery from 2021, created using ArcGIS software by Esri. Overlay data are from MIRTA, GeoBase, FlamMap, LANDFIRE, and RAND geospatial analysis.

Figure 3.12. Installation D Baseline Wildfire Exposure with Phase 2 of Solar Panel Project Outlined

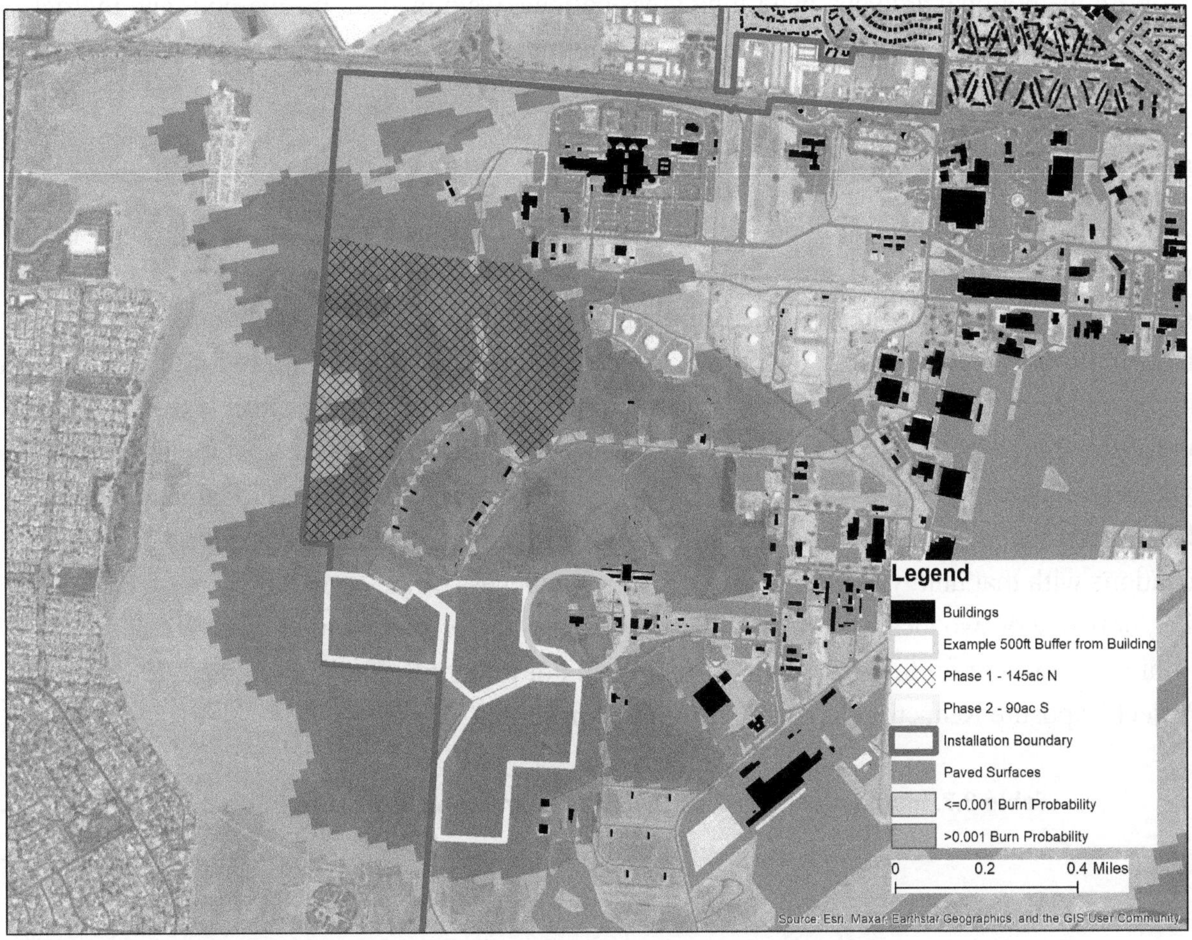

SOURCES: Map features Maxar imagery from 2021, created using ArcGIS software by Esri. Overlay data are from MIRTA, GeoBase, FlamMap, LANDFIRE, and RAND geospatial analysis.

In summary, this section demonstrated with notional examples how to assess the benefiting area of the following:

- a building-scale modernization project that may or may not have been proposed specifically to address resilience (structural flood mitigation at Installation A)
- a new asset to reduce the burn probability near many buildings (structural wildfire mitigation at Installation A)
- mid-sized perimeter interventions that create a new boundary to limit hazard extent (interventional flood and wildfire mitigations at Installation B)
- an engineered exposure mitigation project affecting a substantial portion of the installation (landscape-based flood mitigation at Installation C)
- a large-scale project resulting in substantial land use change that may have incidental impacts for exposure (landscape-based wildfire mitigation at Installation D)
- a phased project (wildfire mitigation at Installation D).

45

Step 3—Describe the Project's Exposure Reduction Potential

With the notional projects' benefiting areas defined, we now describe methods and metrics for estimating the projects' resilience benefits in terms of their potential to reduce hazard exposure.

Installation A Flood Project Exposure Results

Installation A's structural flood project consolidates the functions in four buildings in the benefiting area into a new facility outside the floodplain (not shown in Figure 3.1). Although four buildings were consolidated based on their communication function, only three fall within the benefiting area assessed for the project. Table 3.7 shows that the project reduced exposure for all the buildings owned by the installation's communications support squadron type. In addition, one highly mission-critical (as measured by TMDI) asset belonging to the operations squadron type is no longer exposed. As shown in the last column of Table 3.7, the notional uniqueness of the communications support unit type is low, owing to the fact that there are at least 11 other locations with that unit type (see Table 3.1). The uniqueness of the operations unit type is high (i.e., only one or two locations with that unit type), and the project would reduce but not eliminate exposure for the highly unique unit type. For more information, see the "Additional Project Exposure Reduction Results" section in Appendix C.

Table 3.7. Installation A Project Benefits from Flood Exposure Reductions

Generalized Squadron Type	Number of Benefiting Assets (Pre-'77, '77–'02, Post-'02)	Percentage of Exposed Assets Benefited	PRV of Benefiting Assets (Pre-'77, '77–'02, Post-'02)	TMDI			(Notional) Unit Type Uniqueness of Reduced Exposure
				Number of Benefiting Assets >=80	Number of Benefited Assets with > Brief Interruptability	Number of Benefited Assets with > Extremely Difficult Replicability	
Communications Support	2 (1,0,1)	100	$11.9M (6.0,0,5.9)	1	1	1	L
Operations	1 (1,0,0)	3	$7.1M (7.1,0,0)	1	1	1	H
Total	**3 (2,0,1)**	**3**	**$19.0M (13.1,0,5.9)**	**2**	**2**	**2**	**N/A**

SOURCE: DCAT, RPAD, GeoBase, TMDI, RAND geospatial analysis, and RAND analysis of DRSS-S data.

To assess the project's benefit relative to the installation's baseline exposure conditions, we compare four variables in two charts—first, the percentage of assets exposed versus the number of exposed assets, and second, the number of exposed assets by their replicability versus their interruptability—each by generalized squadron type. For example, in Figure 3.13 the small-scale structural project (communications facility relocation) at Installation A significantly reduces the fraction of the communications squadron type's assets that are exposed to flood, but its effect on other metrics (total number of exposed assets, and assets with low interruptability and/or replicability) is modest.

Figure 3.13. Installation A Communications and Operations Squadron Types' Benefits from Flood Exposure Reduction

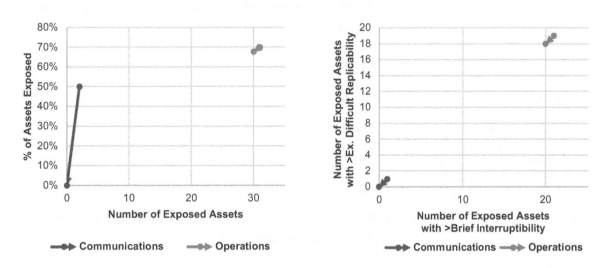

Installation A Wildfire Project Exposure Results

Similar tables and graphics based on the benefiting areas of the other projects can be generated to facilitate comparison across projects. As shown in Table 3.8 and Figure 3.14, Installation A's new auxiliary fire station project benefits eight total assets, including some that account for more than one-half of the maintenance squadron type's exposure. However, a wildfire that ignites in this coverage area may spread beyond the 1,000-meter response radius, meaning that additional assets outside the benefiting area in this notional example may benefit under other conditions. In this example, we do not include unit type uniqueness values as the project does not completely remove all exposure for an individual unit.

Table 3.8. Installation A Project Benefits from Wildfire Exposure Reductions

Generalized Squadron Type	Number of Benefiting Assets	Percentage of Exposed Assets Benefited	PRV of Benefiting Assets	TMDI		
				Number of Benefiting Assets >=80	Number of Benefited Assets with > Brief Interruptability	Number of Benefited Assets with > Extremely Difficult Replicability
Logistics and Readiness	2	22	$8.7M	—	—	2
Maintenance	5	56	$13.9M	1	1	1
Security Forces	1	14	$0.2M	—	—	—
Total	**8**	**15**	**$22.8M**	**1**	**1**	**3**

SOURCE: RPAD, GeoBase, TMDI, FlamMap, LANDFIRE, and RAND geospatial analysis.
NOTE: All buildings were built before 2006.

Figure 3.14. Installation A Logistics, Maintenance, and Security Squadron Types' Benefits from Wildfire Exposure Reduction

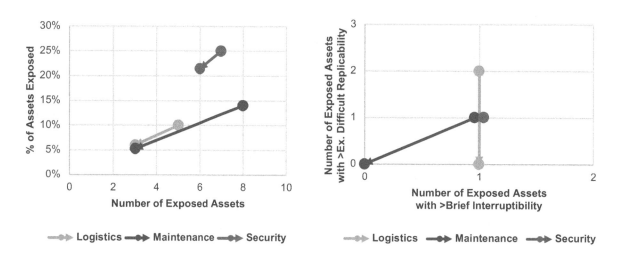

NOTE: Maintenance and security squadron types' exposed assets for interruptability jittered for visual clarity.

For more information on other projects described in Step 2 above, see the "Additional Project Exposure Reduction Results" section of Appendix C.

Step 4—Compare Projects Based on Potential Resilience Benefits

Comparing Metrics

Quantifying the exposure reduction benefit relative to a baseline level exposure provides details to inform decisions about which projects, either within a single installation or between installations, might be the most competitive candidates for funding and execution. Figures 3.13 and 3.14 and Tables 3.7 and 3.8 are intended as tools for presenting standardized data and exposure reduction metrics for a given project. However, such data can only inform prioritization decisions rather than definitively determine which projects should be selected for execution. Moving beyond simple metrics toward project prioritization thus requires subjective interpretation of a project's potential benefits in the context of mission objectives.

Figure 3.15 illustrates how three notional projects might compare in the decision space bounded by two metrics presented above: (1) number of high-TMDI assets and (2) PRV. Projects that perform poorly across both metrics are easy to sideline (Project 1). However, comparing projects that perform well on different metrics (Projects 2 and 3) requires a choice regarding how to weight the metrics. This is further complicated by additional information about the value of some projects in the context of the broader enterprise (i.e., Project 3's benefit to highly unique unit types). As indicated in our unit slack analysis above, a project that reduces exposure for a highly unique unit could be prioritized over another project that reduces exposure for low-uniqueness units. If multiple projects reduce exposure for highly unique units, a decisionmaker may then consider whether specific unit types or missions should be prioritized.

Figure 3.15. Notional Comparison of Project Benefits

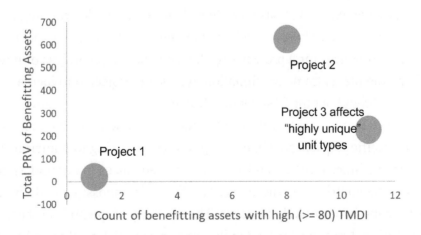

Below are some examples of choices decisionmakers might face that are informed by the outputs of the previous three steps but ultimately require the decisionmaker's judgment:

- whether to maximize exposure reduction benefits for units (or mission functions or any other grouping of choice) with the largest absolute number of assets benefiting from a

49

project or those with the greatest benefit relative to their total asset portfolio at an installation

- whether to favor projects that reduce some exposure across several units or projects that eliminate exposure entirely for one unit type
- whether to favor projects that reduce risk to total exposed PRV over those that primarily reduce risk to high-TMDI assets
- whether to prioritize exposure of unique functions not easily replicated at other installations
- how the loss of function of even a single asset may have impacts far beyond that implied by criticality metrics such as TMDI.

Climate Uncertainty

One aspect of project prioritization in which such judgment will become increasingly important in the coming decades is the assessment of exposure risk stemming from climate uncertainty. Current DAF guidance for minimizing hazard risk at installations is based in part on historical exposure trends that are likely to change as climate-related hazards intensify. For example, guidance that limits construction within the historical 100-year floodplain (1 percent AEP) may fail to sufficiently mitigate risk if such flood events begin to occur more frequently in the future. The uncertainty around the rate of increase in the frequency and severity of climate-driven hazards complicates the development of new standards to account for such changes. In addition, climate uncertainty may mask the possibility that some hazards, such as ice storms, may become less severe in the future because of climate change. Thus, planning for long-term climate resilience should be done with this uncertainty in mind.

The analysis described in Steps 1–3 assumes baseline hazard scenarios for flood (1 percent AEP) and wildfire based on environmental conditions that approximate the historical climatic regime. Which assets are exposed at baseline (Step 1) is central to determining the resilience afforded by any given project. Thus, any shift in the underlying baseline exposure scenario could have significant consequences for a project's resilience benefits, regardless of how the metrics are weighted. For example, extreme precipitation events are projected to increase in many areas of the United States throughout the 21st century because of global temperature rise.[86] Although the scientific evidence that this trend will lead to increased flood exposure risk has been well established,[87] the specific impacts are challenging to predict, owing to numerous physical and methodological uncertainties (see Appendix D). Despite advances in our understanding of the physical processes that contribute to these uncertainties, it is impossible to definitively predict which climatic scenario is most likely to occur. This inability to quantify probabilities of different climate futures limits our understanding of exposure risk to climate hazards, and therefore, also limits our confidence that a particular project will realize its expected resilience

---

[86] USGCRP, 2018, Chapter 2, Key Message 6.

[87] USGCRP, 2018, Chapter 2, Key Message 1.

benefits. Thus, resilience project prioritization falls into the realm of "decisionmaking under deep uncertainty" when considering future climate conditions.[88]

Global climate models (GCMs) are often used to understand potential future changes in hazard exposure.[89] As projections from these models have inherent uncertainty (Appendix D), any analysis that relies on inputs from GCM projections must be interpreted with this uncertainty in mind. This is particularly relevant for large-scale installation projects and for projects in which the asset is required to last for many decades, given that the uncertainty in climate models and their assumptions increases as we look further out into the future. It is also relevant when the hazard in question is one where the climate models themselves do not generally perform well at reproducing observed patterns of exposure, such as flooding.

When considering the candidate flood resilience projects, climate uncertainty may cause the actual level of exposure to be different from the level expected based on the initial exposure risk calculation. This can affect how one approaches the task of project prioritization. For example, the baseline flood exposure presented here is based on the 1 percent AEP driven by the precipitation projections used in the DCAT. This probability is calculated based on historical frequencies of precipitation events—specifically, the "100-year storm," or rainfall levels that have a 1 percent probability of occurring in any given year. Because the 1 percent AEP is a statistical representation of reality, it is not absolute. It is possible that assets in the floodplain will experience a flood of this severity more frequently than once every 100 years. However, it is also uncertain how much more frequently the historical 100-year storm could occur in the future. Therefore, if one were to execute a project on the assumption that its resilience value will increase in the future because of climate-driven increases in exposure at that installation, this expected resilience value may never be realized if future exposure remains close to baseline levels. Conversely, projects that score low on resilience metrics based on current levels of exposure may be underestimated if one fails to account for the possibility that future exposure at that installation may be significantly higher than expected.

Accounting for climate uncertainty when prioritizing projects does not guarantee that projects will realize their expected resilience value in the face of future exposure. However, it can offer an additional layer of information to consider when comparing projects whose resilience metrics are otherwise fairly similar, or high in different metrics (per discussion above). In general, projects that stand to do better when considering climate uncertainty have the following characteristics:

- **They offer resilience against hazards whose key climatic drivers have low uncertainty of future increased exposure.** For example, climate science indicates with high confidence that "a warmer climate will intensify very wet and very dry weather and

---

[88] Robert J. Lempert, Steven W. Popper, and Steven C. Bankes, *Shaping the Next One Hundred Years: New Methods for Quantitative, Long-Term Policy Analysis*, RAND Corporation, MR-1626-RPC, 2003.

[89] Pinson et al., 2021.

climate events and seasons, with implications for flooding or drought."[90] As wildfires are more likely to occur during extreme dry periods and floods are driven by extreme precipitation events, projects that target either of these hazards could receive additional consideration over other projects that would enhance resilience against hazards whose future trajectories are less certain, such as hail, ice storms, dust storms, heavy snowfall, and landslides.[91]

- **They have interventions that are flexible to changing conditions.** For example, deployable flood barriers (Installation B) may be moved and/or expanded to adapt to changes in severity and location of flooding at the base. In contrast, if the new site selected for the communications relocation and/or consolidation project (Installation A) were to be flooded by an extreme precipitation event outside the range of projected hazard severity, its benefiting area could be reduced to zero.

Both considerations require a "human in the loop" to assess whether the additional priority conferred on some projects due to accounting for climate uncertainty enables them to compete with other projects that fare better according to metric-based measures alone. In any case, we acknowledge that there is likely no single approach that is sufficiently robust to capture all relevant considerations for selecting one project above others. This requires decisionmakers to take an adaptive risk-based approach that considers trade-offs, values, and risk tolerance in a variety of future conditions.

Limitations

We have sought to limit the fidelity of the analysis to what existing data allow to ensure the usability of the proposed approach for the DAF. Therefore, the framework has several limitations, which we describe here.

First, it was outside the scope of our framework to compare a project's climate resilience benefits against other objectives and priorities it may address—a task more aptly handled via stakeholder discussions.

Second, the framework is intended to serve only as a screening tool for projects with potential climate resilience value. For projects that appear to perform well across the metrics included in the framework, additional analyses that consider local conditions, more-granular representations of exposure (e.g., flood depths and not just extents), and engineering constraints will need to be conducted before funding decisions are made.

Third, the data and methods underlying the framework are not without limitations. Although the methods and limitations of DCAT's riverine flooding analysis are well documented,[92] there are also important caveats to consider when using FlamMap to estimate wildfire exposure risk.

---

[90] IPCC, 2021.

[91] While extreme heat and low precipitation are key climate drivers for wildfire, other environmental factors with relatively greater uncertainty also contribute to wildfire, such as wind speed and fuel moisture. IPCC, 2021.

[92] Pinson et al., 2021.

Our FlamMap model relies on a landscape file built on public data (e.g., LANDFIRE) that may not be kept current as wildfires, climate change, development, and other natural or anthropogenic processes drive bioconversion in wildland fuel models.[93] FlamMap takes weather and fuel moisture parameters from the user and assumes that they will remain constant.[94] We chose conditions—red-flag wind speeds and very dry fuel moistures—to simulate an environment that is fire prone but relatively within norms. However, it is possible that more-intense wildfire conditions will occur in the future because of climate change. Choosing such an approach requires a decision to be made about the simulated conditions—should modelers pursue a severe-but-plausible scenario, as we did, or something more extreme? In addition, FlamMap does not consider such factors as wildfire suppression efforts—a key component of both fire spread and asset vulnerability, but one that is difficult to model given limited availability of information on both DAF firefighting resources suitable for wildland fire management and the presence of nearby cooperating agencies or departments with which DAF or individual facilities have mutual aid or other agreements.[95] Despite these limitations, both DCAT and FlamMap are reasonable sources of hazard exposure information of the sort needed to screen projects based on their potential climate resilience value.

Fourth, the framework does not explicitly account for project costs or other attributes that influence investment decisions. Such information could be introduced in Step 4 of the framework to further contextualize the comparison of metrics and inform decisions about metric weighting.

---

[93] Rob C. Seli, Stuart Brittan, and Chuck W. McHugh, "FlamMap Online Help, version 6.0," available from within the FlamMap application, 2019; Matthew G. Rollins, Brendan C. Ward, Greg Dillon, Sarah Pratt, and Ann Wolf, "Developing the LANDFIRE Fire Regime Data Products," U.S. Department of Agriculture Forest Service Rocky Mountain Research Station, Intermountain Fire Sciences Laboratory, 2007.

[94] Seli, Brittan, and McHugh, 2019.

[95] Interagency Fuel Treatment Decision Support System Help Center, "Technical Documentation—Landscape Burn Probability with FlamMap," undated.

Chapter 4. Resilience Investment Decisionmaking in Other Organizations

To further support our analysis of how the Air Force can assess and prioritize investments in building infrastructure resilience to climate change, we sought to understand how other organizations approach this same challenge. Given the relative newness of such considerations in infrastructure investment-making, we aimed to identify where other organizations stand in developing their own processes and assessments for making these types of investment decisions. In doing so, we sought to ensure that the framework that we present in Chapter 3 did not already exist in some form in the practices and processes of other organizations and that the framework did not omit any important elements found in the approaches of these organizations. Our intent was to identify commonalities and unique approaches from these organizations to provide the Air Force with suggestions on how it might structure its processes moving forward. We set out to compare the practices of both governmental and nongovernmental organizations, seeking to offer a diverse set of approaches from which the Air Force might learn. We focused on five comparison organizations to ensure that our analysis remained within the scope and timeline of our research. We selected the following organizations to serve as comparison cases:

- other military service: Army
- federal agencies: National Park Service (NPS) and FEMA (BRIC program)
- private sector: FedEx and Google.

How We Selected the Comparison Organizations

We sought to provide the Air Force with insights from comparison organizations that featured both similar and different characteristics from the Air Force. We hoped this approach would offer both relatable and out-of-the-box comparisons to ensure a variety of perspectives. First, we developed a list of organizational characteristics to serve as the criteria for selection. Second, we cultivated the list of selection criteria by conducting a review of past RAND research that compared a military service (i.e., the Air Force, Army, Navy, or Marine Corps) with external organizations in some manner. Third, from this review, we compiled a list of common criteria used to determine comparison cases, and then discussed this list with subject-matter experts (SMEs) on our team and solicited their feedback to ensure that we were not missing criteria relevant to the Air Force. Fourth and finally, with their feedback incorporated, we down-selected to a final list of four main criteria most related to the Air Force. The criteria we used to choose relevant comparison cases were:

- **geographical distribution**: the organization maintains locations throughout the United States and/or globally

- **infrastructure management**: the organization has ownership, operation, and maintenance of extensive physical infrastructure
- **organization type**: the organization includes both public- and private-sector representatives
- **transportation role**: the organization conducts some form of transportation of goods and/or people.

All our organizations met at least two of the criteria, which meant that the organizations ranged from very similar to somewhat similar to the Air Force. To ensure that we did not wholly focus on organizations that were like the Air Force, we purposely included cases that differed in major ways. For instance, we particularly included FEMA as an example of an organization that was not making investments in its own infrastructure but rather running a program that evaluated projects for investment. We also included Google because it provided a private representative with a global presence, but the company maintains a smaller amount of infrastructure compared with the Air Force and does not provide transportation services.

Aspects of the comparison cases created limitations that affected the extent of our analysis. First, the organizations we chose had to have publicly available and shareable information for the analysis. We could not compare organizations that did not disclose information related to investment decisionmaking because of classification or proprietary concerns. We were also limited to the information provided in public documents for those organizations that we were unable to speak with directly. Second, our private-sector comparison organizations were less open to interviews, so we relied entirely on the public documents provided by the companies on their environmental programs. Third, some of the comparison organizations' processes, especially those in private industry, include a broader understanding of climate and may include considerations related to sustainability or environmental, social, and governance (ESG) concepts. We considered these to still be close comparisons with specific processes related to building infrastructure resilience because of climate change but note that they are not exact comparisons. Fourth, the timing and scope of our project limited us to five organizations.

On a related note, our analysis focuses on the processes that organizations use to evaluate, prioritize, and select infrastructure projects that incorporate climate change considerations. Consequently, we do not include discussions of the outcomes of these processes or attempt to evaluate their performance for three main reasons. First, we wished to understand how organizations think about and decide on which projects to invest in to assist the DAF in building and improving its own processes. Second, like the DAF, many of our comparison organizations are in the early stages of developing prioritization and decisionmaking processes and thus have not established assessment mechanisms to determine whether those processes have yet to meet desired outcomes. Finally, even after organizations have implemented their processes and are at a stage in which these processes are mature enough to evaluate, uncertainties related to climate impacts on specific locations and infrastructure complicate assessments of whether processes led to desired outcomes. It is difficult to definitively link projects' alterations to improved outcomes and thus show that processes led to the best project selections.

We conducted our research and analysis of the comparison organizations in two primary ways. First, we performed a detailed review of each organization's strategic, policy, process and/or environmental documents. During this review, we assessed the documents by systematically applying the following questions:

- What processes, if any, does the organization employ to evaluate, prioritize, and invest in projects related to building infrastructure resilience to climate change?
- Which entities in the organization play a role in these processes? How do they interact to make investment decisions?
- Are climate resilience considerations incorporated into existing infrastructure investment processes, or do organizations use separate processes and/or sources of funding to address climate resilience?

Second, we sought to speak with either representatives of the selected organizations or SMEs on the organizations to extrapolate on what we learned from the document review. We were able to conduct three interviews—two with representatives from the NPS's Climate Research Group and facilities and construction division and one with a SME on the Army and its infrastructure processes. We conducted outreach to FEMA, FedEx, and Google. We were unable to connect with representatives from FEMA and Google, and FedEx declined to speak with us, citing proprietary concerns. Although these interviews may have provided additional information, public documentation about each organization provided enough detail to allow us to identify common practices and insights to complete our analysis.

Climate Resilience Investment Decisionmaking

The following sections present findings from our research on how the five comparison organizations consider and incorporate climate change into their infrastructure investments or investment-making decisions.[96] Generally, each of the following subsections discusses positions, offices, and/or departments that contribute to the investment process, the organization's infrastructure investment evaluation and prioritization process (or steps taken to develop this process if it is still in progress), and how climate change considerations are incorporated into the process.[97] Because each organization is unique and in different stages of developing formal processes and procedures for considering climate change in infrastructure investment, some cases present other specifics to provide as much detail as possible for that particular

---

[96] Our private-sector comparisons, in particular, included examples of processes that looked more broadly at climate and investment-making decisions, often within their company's ESG or sustainability programs.

[97] This step includes how organizations define resilience or climate resilience in their documentation, where available.

organization. Finally, we include a short discussion of how the Army and NPS approach the inherent uncertainty of climate change futures in their processes. [98]

Other Military Service

Army

Similar to the Air Force, the Army is working on developing processes and procedures to incorporate climate change considerations in infrastructure investments. One of the Army's main steps is the development and release of several strategic and policy documents on the significance of climate change and building resilience to its effects over the past few years.[99]

This collection of documents provides information on how the Army is initially thinking about climate resilience in the context of infrastructure investment decisionmaking.[100] The following section compiles these references to identify where the Army is heading with these processes.

Using our review of the documents listed above, the Army has outlined oversight and management responsibilities, determined how climate resilience will be integrated into planning processes, and delineated how those planning efforts will feed into the infrastructure investment process. First, the Army delegated several responsibilities related to incorporating climate resilience into the investment process in Army Directive 2020-08. The directive issues roles and responsibilities to Army leadership for installation policies, processes, and procedures related to addressing climate change.[101] Table 4.1 presents the Army entities and corresponding responsibilities for including climate resilience in infrastructure investment. The items in italics highlight those responsibilities particularly relevant to investment decisions (i.e., resources, funding, budgeting, and execution).

---

[98] We conducted research into the comparison cases' approaches to uncertainty to understand how they consider the rate and magnitude of hazards' impacts on their infrastructure and/or operations. We were able to discover information on uncertainty for only two of our five cases.

[99] The Army's strategic documents focusing on climate change (with full citations) include Department of the Army, *United States Army Climate Strategy*, February 2022; Army Directive 2020-08, *U.S. Army Installation Policy to Address Threats Caused by Changing Climate and Extreme Weather*, Secretary of Defense, September 11, 2020; and Department of the Army, *Army Installations Strategy*, December 2020. In support of these strategic documents, the Army has also released the following planning documents (with full citations): U.S. Army, *Army Installations Strategy Implementation Plan Fiscal Years 2022-2024*, undated; and A. O. Pinson, K. D. White, S. A. Moore, S. D. Samuelson, B. A. Thames, P. S. O'Brien, C. A. Hiemstra, P. M. Loechl, and E. E. Ritchie, *Army Climate Resilience Handbook: Change 1*, U.S. Army Corps of Engineers, August 2020.

[100] The Army defines *resilience* as the "ability to prepare, absorb, recover, and adapt to changed conditions." In the context of infrastructure resilience specifically, the Army states that "for planning purposes, resilience means infrastructure that is designed to anticipate future performance conditions." See Pinson et al., 2020, p. 11.

[101] Army Directive 2020-08, 2020, pp. 2–3.

Table 4.1. Army Roles and Responsibilities for Incorporating Climate Change into Infrastructure Investments

Army Leadership Position	Responsibilities Related to Incorporating Climate Resilience in Infrastructure Investments
Assistant Secretary of the Army (ASA) for Installations, Energy, and the Environment (IE&E)	Maintain oversight of installation climate policy; establish strategic direction for planning, programming, budgeting, and execution of requirements to address climate threats.
Deputy Chief of Staff, G-9	Supervise the execution of the Army installation climate policy; advise ASA IE&E on resourcing and evaluation; develop implementation plan for policy.
Commanders of Army installations	Assess, plan for, and adapt to projected impacts of climate change and extreme weather by adding information from climate prediction tools into facility and infrastructure plans, policies, and procedures.
Senior commanders, landholding commands	Submit requirements for consideration in existing planning, programming, and budgeting requirements and execute resources to address potential threats from climate.
Garrison commanders	Direct master planners to identify range of impacts from climate change that could affect the installation, assess their likelihood, and identify preparedness and resilience measures to mitigate their effects.

SOURCE: Army Directive 2020-08, 2020.

A review of the Army positions and corresponding responsibilities shows how the Army is trying to make Army leaders at all levels accountable for integrating different aspects of climate resilience into infrastructure investment-making processes.

The Army's Process: Planning Steps Lead Up to Investment-Making

As stated, the Army issued multiple documents related to climate change in the past couple of years, primarily focusing on strategy and planning. Consequently, how the Army specifically incorporates climate resilience into their infrastructure investment process has not yet been outlined in a public source. However, the *Army Climate Resilience Handbook*, while focusing on integrating climate change into planning efforts, provides context and links to the investment-making process. The handbook delineates four main steps for addressing climate change in the planning process. Of the four steps, the final step offers some context for how the Army might identify and consider climate resilience–related projects. During this step, the handbook directs planners to collect and report on installation areas at risk because of climate change and adaptive measures to address those risks (i.e., potential climate resilience projects). The intended outcome of the fourth step is a catalog of options for climate mitigation and resilience for each installation. The potential options are to be organized by hazard type, structural, nonstructural, and natural/nature-based solutions. The handbook instructs planners to continually update the catalog of options as new data emerges, so selections can be made as "funding or other opportunities become available."[102] As a planning document, the handbook ends at this step, but

---

[102] Pinson et al., 2020, pp. 59–62.

the options developed from the planning processes likely feed into the list of projects that the Army will consider for future investment.

The Army is currently developing its formal process for incorporating climate change into infrastructure investments.[103] The Army has integrated sustainability into installation planning and implementation for several years, which has some overlap with climate-related considerations. However, the Army seeks to move beyond existing policy and incorporate climate change more fully and specifically into infrastructure investment decisionmaking.[104] The *Army Installations Strategy Implementation Plan Fiscal Years 2022–2024* provides a few insights into how the Army intends to do so.[105] Under the Army implementation plan's strategic objective of adopting resilient systems, the Army plans to "develop a return-on-investment (ROI) model that benchmarks insurance industry examples to enable the Army installation enterprise to price the value of resilience investments, including investments that address climate risks."[106] The completion date for the ROI model is the end of fiscal year 2023. The implementation plan also notes that climate-specific tasks and outcomes will be addressed in a forthcoming *Army Climate Strategy Implementation Plan*.[107] Stating the intent to develop a separate implementation plan dedicated specifically to climate change shows that the Army is working to attain its goal of more fully incorporating climate change into decisionmaking processes, including in investments. At the time of writing this report, the *Army Climate Strategy Implementation Plan* had not yet been released. Once the implementation plan has been issued, the Air Force may wish to review the report to learn how the Army outlines its investment-making processes.

Federal Agencies

The National Park Service

The NPS's mission is to "preserve unimpaired the natural and cultural resources of the National Park System for the enjoyment, education, and inspiration of this and future generations"; therefore, incorporating climate change into the maintenance of its extensive infrastructure is a crucial part of meeting that mission. The NPS's collection of infrastructure includes 423 units (typically referred to as *parks*) covering 850 million acres and 150 other related areas across the United States.[108] Consequently, the NPS currently aims to establish the inclusion of climate change in its planning and investment decisions, and sharing relevant

---

[103] This assessment is based on the context provided in the Army's climate planning and strategy documents and information provided during our interview with an Army SME on July 5, 2022.

[104] Army SME, interview with authors, July 5, 2022.

[105] U.S. Army, undated.

[106] U.S. Army, undated, p. 10.

[107] U.S. Army, undated, pp. 30–31.

[108] NPS, "Our Mission," webpage, undated-b; NPS, "National Park System—Units/Parks," webpage, undated-a.

information on climate change, as consistent practices across the agency. The agency encourages park units to consider climate change impacts in every infrastructure investment, making it part and parcel of its existing investment decisionmaking processes. As one interviewee noted, "We feel like it is part of the world we live in now. [Climate change] needs to be a part of what we do."[109] Information-sharing plays a large role in increasing the agency's standardization of the considerations of climate change in infrastructure. One aspect of this information sharing is an effort to develop uniform definitions of key terms related to climate. The NPS's Climate Change Response Program developed a taxonomy of words and phrases that can be applied by all programs making climate-related decisions, including those in infrastructure.[110]

NPS's Processes Part I: The Bureau Investment Review Board Process for Enterprise-Level Decisionmaking

For large-scale infrastructure projects, the NPS incorporates climate change into an existing investment decisionmaking process. These projects, which are defined as costing more than $1 million, are now required to use climate data and information to inform investment decisions. The NPS's standard practice is to evaluate large projects on a case-by-case basis. Project managers at individual park units develop infrastructure project proposals for consideration by an enterprise-level group, known as the Bureau Investment Review Board (BIRB). The board consists of 12 high-level senior executive service members both from within the service and from external agencies.[111]

As part of the BIRB process, managers of proposed infrastructure projects must show how a project's design accommodates future climate projections. Although projects are developed and evaluated on a per-asset basis, the proposals also attempt to show, when applicable, the broader impact that a project could have if implemented. This includes any benefits that may extend beyond the designated asset, whether to the broader park unit or community beyond. The BIRB takes these potential impacts into consideration when making investment decisions. During the review process, the BIRB works with SMEs, including those within the NPS's Climate Change Response Program and park design engineers, to ensure that relevant climate projections and information are appropriately incorporated into design proposals. In terms of determining whether one project should be prioritized over another based on its park unit, the NPS does not have a hierarchy of park units because they are all individually protected. Yet to capture some of the potential differences between park unit proposals, the NPS applies an asset priority index

---

[109] NPS official, interview with authors, June 3, 2022.

[110] NPS official, interview with authors, June 3, 2022.

[111] NPS members come from across the service and include the NPS comptroller, associate directors of enterprise level offices, regional directors of park units, and park superintendents. Two external representatives come from federal or state agencies. Five of the board positions are held by permanent members, while seven others rotate on three-year terms (NPS official, interview with authors, June 3, 2022; Briefing materials provided to the authors, April 2022).

(API) measure. The API is calculated and maintained at the individual unit level, within the NPS's Facility Management Software System. The API uses several criteria to help inform prioritization of assets, including criticality to the NPS and/or park unit mission, safety for visitor use, and historical importance, among others.[112]

Before the BIRB reviews proposed infrastructure projects, the projects have been assessed at the individual unit and regional levels. The board typically reviews projects first at the concept phase to determine whether they should receive initial approval and funding. After approved projects progress through early stages of development, the BIRB reviews projects a second time during the authorization phase. Project managers present a more comprehensive design proposal, including more-specific climate projections and considerations, especially compared with the initial concept application. Although this is the current procedure, NPS officials noted during our interviews that it is developing methods for incorporating more-detailed climate and environmental considerations in the process as early as possible. For instance, the current process employs a natural hazard checklist that covers basic information about the types of hazards a proposed project could help address and/or should consider when developing design characteristics. The BIRB currently reviews this list and has informal discussions regarding the information presented in proposal packages. However, the BIRB intends to develop a more comprehensive and formal assessment of climate-related questions by applying an established set of criteria for evaluation.[113]

Once the BIRB receives the project proposals from NPS regional offices, the members individually review the proposals and then collectively discuss, debate, and make final recommendations. When considering each proposed project, the BIRB seeks to address two main questions:

- Does the project support or contribute to the park unit's stated mission?
- Is the project financially and environmentally feasible?

The BIRB specifically deliberates the project's climate considerations in the second question. Once the BIRB completes its evaluation of a project, it comes to one of three main decisions. First, a project is approved fully, accepting all provisions as delineated in the proposal. Second, a project is approved, but the BIRB requires that certain conditions or stipulations be met before the project can move forward. Third, the project proposal is not accepted and must be revised completely for resubmission and assessment by the BIRB.[114]

---

[112] NPS official, interview with authors, June 3, 2022.

[113] The BIRB is also working to develop a set of support tools for park managers who create and present infrastructure project proposals. In doing so, managers aim to make the proposals more standardized across the NPS, with the same analyses completed for each project before they are submitted for review (NPS facilities officials, interview with the authors, July 7, 2022).

[114] NPS facilities officials, interview with authors, July 7, 2022.

Although the NPS recognizes that climate change needs to be integrated into every infrastructure investment decision moving forward, and thus has found ways to ensure its inclusion in standard investment processes, the NPS also acknowledges that certain conditions may increase the potential for climate hazards across common types of park units. As a result, it is developing a specific approach to investing in infrastructure in coastal park units because of their increased vulnerability to flooding and extreme weather events due to climate change. Known as the Coastal Investment Decision Framework, the initiative would enable a broader, portfolio-based investment approach for park assets at coastal units. The NPS intends to apply the framework to compare potential options in the "coastal asset" portfolio, as it recognizes that the increasing impacts of climate change mean that these units may not be able to maintain all assets in the same manner as they have in the past. Choices of which coastal assets receive priority will need to be made, and this framework aims to help park and system managers make these kinds of decisions.[115]

The creators of the Coastal Investment Decision Framework seek to provide a set of standard criteria to be applied by all park units in coastal settings. The framework would help the units' personnel decide in which projects to invest based on their unique circumstances. The criteria would be based on projections of sea level rise and associated hazards, such as storms and erosions. Although the framework is still a work in progress, the NPS developed an initial set of criteria for the framework, which include

- vulnerability of the unit to identified hazards
- importance and function of the unit
- historical significance of the unit
- projected amount of seal level rise
- cost of the proposed project.

Additional factors are still under consideration and may be added to this list as the framework develops. NPS intends to deploy the framework at multiple levels of the organization—the individual park unit level, the regional level, and the service level. Assessment entities, like the BIRB, could use the framework to inform their investment decisions for coastal assets as well. Although the initiative specifically targets certain types of projects (i.e., those addressing coastal hazards), the NPS is considering employing the framework in standing plans and processes, where appropriate.[116]

---

[115] Park Planning, Facilities, and Lands Directorate, 2022; NPS official, email to authors, June 5, 2022; NPS official, interview with authors, June 3, 2022.

[116] For instance, the NPS may include the framework as a tool in its facility investment plans (Park Planning, Facilities, and Lands Directorate, 2022; "Developing an Evaluation Framework to Inform NPS Coastal Infrastructure Investment Decisions," notes sent by an NPS official via email after an interview with authors, June 3, 2022).

FEMA's BRIC program aims to make proactive investments in the resilience of state, local, tribal, and territorial communities across the United States. The program seeks to shift the typical approach of the federal government to address disasters and natural hazards to one that is proactive rather than reactive. The FEMA BRIC program awards funding to community projects "for natural hazard mitigation activities that promote climate adaptation and resilience with respect to those hazards."[117] The BRIC program represents a unique comparison case because it is not a program run for a federal agency but rather by a federal agency for external entities. Consequently, it has a detailed process for assessing, prioritizing, and selecting projects. One other additional distinction is important to note. The BRIC program focuses on mitigating natural hazards and recognizes that there are "growing hazards associated with climate change."[118] However, FEMA grants awards for projects that address natural hazards writ large, not just those attributable to or associated with climate change.[119] Thus, the following synopsis of the BRIC program's process can provide helpful insights into how to think about prioritizing infrastructure investments, because that is the program's entire purpose. However, it will not provide the same types of insights that a program focused solely on climate change and carried out by a federal entity for its own investment purposes might.

Process for Evaluating and Selecting BRIC Projects

The BRIC program defines *resilience* as "The ability to prepare for and adapt to changing conditions and withstand and recover rapidly from disruptions. Resilience includes the ability to withstand and recover from deliberate attacks, accidents, or naturally occurring threats or incidents."[120] Although this definition is broad in that it includes attacks and accidents, the BRIC program focuses primarily on natural disasters and hazards.

Since the inaugural year of the BRIC program in 2020, U.S. communities seeking grants for hazard mitigation projects apply through the program's annual Notice of Funding Opportunity (NOFO). The following section describes the process for the national program, which represents most of the funding granted by the BRIC initiative.[121] In the BRIC application process, states serve as applicants and organize local community proposals, which are labeled *subapplicants*.

---

[117] FEMA, "About BRIC: Reducing Risk Through Hazard Mitigation," webpage, undated; FEMA, 2021a, p. 3.

[118] FEMA, 2021a, p. 3.

[119] FEMA, 2021a, p. 4.

[120] FEMA, *Resources for Climate Resilience*, December 2021e, p. 3. FEMA notes that this definition comes from the National Institute of Standards and Technology, *Risk Management Framework for Information Systems and Organizations: A System Life Cycle Approach for Security and Privacy*, Joint Task Force, NIST SP 800-37, revision 2, December 2018.

[121] The BRIC program also awards funding to states, territories, and tribes, through separately allocated funds. Of the $1 billion available through the FY21 NOFO, the national competition had $919 million to grant. See FEMA, 2021a, p. 6.

The project proposals proceed through three different levels of evaluation, contingent on approval and type of application. The first step is assessing whether a subapplicant meets required eligibility and proposal completeness criteria. Once past this initial step, the subapplication moves on to additional review using a set of technical criteria.[122] The technical criteria each have designated quantitative scores as follows:

- project addresses infrastructure (20 points)
- project mitigates risk to one or more community lifelines (15 points)
- project incorporates nature-based solutions (10 points)
- project applicant has a tribal-, territorial-, or statewide building code adoption:

  - applicant uses 2015 version of International Building or Residential Code (10 points)
  - applicant uses 2018 or 2021 version of International Building or Residential Code (20 points)

- project "generated from previous FEMA [Hazard Mitigation Assistance (HMA)] Advance Assistance . . . , High Hazard Potential Dams (HHPD) award, or DHS Cybersecurity and Infrastructure Security Agency's (CISA) Regional Resiliency Assessment Program (RRAP), or the subapplicant is a past recipient of BRIC nonfinancial Direct Technical Assistance" (20 points)
- "a non-federal cost share of at least 30% (or, for Economically Disadvantaged Rural Communities . . . at least 12%)." To receive full points; federal cost share cannot be more than 70 percent (5 points)
- project applicant designated as an economically disadvantaged rural community (15 points.[123]

For almost all technical criteria, FEMA implements a binary application for the associated scores, so projects that meet a criterion receive full scores for that criterion, while projects that do not, receive no credit. The eight technical criteria, described in Figure 4.1, focus on the impact to the applicant community, the risks and types of mitigation addressed by the project, adherence to specific building codes, previous project funding, and cost considerations.[124]

In addition to the assessment and scoring based on the technical criteria, FEMA evaluates successful subapplications with a set of qualitative criteria. Depending on the number of applications submitted to the BRIC program, FEMA may use the technical criteria review as a priority screening tool for the qualitative criteria review. It may also take into consideration the state applicant's ranking of its local projects in the FEMA BRIC application system (FEMA GO). According to the 2021 NOFO, at least one subapplicant proposal from each applicant will be submitted for qualitative review. FEMA includes the qualitative criteria review as a method of

---

[122] The technical criteria "offer incentives for elements valued by FEMA." FEMA, 2021a, p. 26.

[123] FEMA, 2021a, p. 27.

[124] FEMA, *BRIC Technical Criteria*, FEMA program support material, August 2022, pp.1–6; FEMA, 2021a, pp. 26–28.

providing applicants the opportunity to supply more-detailed information about their proposed project.[125]

There are six qualitative criteria, and each is assigned a point amount as follows:

- The application "details how the project will . . . reduce risk and increase resilience . . . , realize ancillary benefits, and leverage innovation" (35 points).
- The application shows "how the project will enhance climate adaptation and resilience . . . [and] how the project is . . . responsive to the effects of climate change . . . and/or other future conditions" (20 points).
- The application is able to show how the projects will manage costs and schedule, how the project will be implemented, and how innovative techniques will be incorporated (15 points).
- The application is able to demonstrate the project's communitywide benefits and the proportion of the population that will be affected; it also outlines how the project will minimize negative impacts and maximize positive ones (25 points).
- The application describes the project's planned outreach strategy and supporting activities to the community to advance mitigation (5 points).
- The application incorporates partnerships to ensure that the project meets community needs, including helping disadvantaged communities, and shows the outcomes of said partnerships (15 points).[126]

Unlike with the technical criteria, subapplicants can receive partial credit for the qualitative criteria, as FEMA allocates points on a graded scale.[127] Of relevance to our research, one of the BRIC program's qualitative criteria focuses on climate change. The "climate change and other future conditions" category asks the applicants to detail how their project will "enhance climate adaptation and resilience," and is "responsive to the effects of climate change and other conditions" using relevant data sources. This category has the third-highest point amount (20) of the six qualitative criteria.[128]

FEMA prioritizes the proposed projects based on the cumulative scores that they receive from their technical and qualitative reviews. FEMA ranks the projects based on their scores, using the priority ranking to determine which projects receive funding for the given program year. FEMA may choose to fund a project outside this priority ranking based on four characteristics, (1) availability of funding; (2) duplication of subapplications; (3) program priorities and policy factors, such as the anticipated benefits to disadvantaged communities; and (4) other relevant information like past performance on other FEMA grants.[129] Thus, FEMA

---

[125] FEMA, 2021a, pp. 26, 28–29.

[126] FEMA, 2021a, pp. 28–29.

[127] To evaluate projects based on the qualitative criteria, FEMA convenes a National Review Panel. The panel consists of representatives from federal agencies and state, local, tribal, and territorial partners.

[128] FEMA, 2021d, pp. 1–9; FEMA, 2021a, pp. 28–29, 31.

[129] FEMA, 2021a, p. 31.

selects projects based on their technical and qualitative scores, and potential additional criteria, when applicable.

Private Sector

We included two cases from outside the federal government to ensure a diversity of perspectives and approaches to inform the Air Force's infrastructure investment decisionmaking processes. FedEx, a shipping company with a global presence, shares similar characteristics with the Air Force. To delineate FedEx and Google's processes, we reviewed their ESG reports, global citizenship reports, and submissions to the Carbon Disclosure Project (CDP). Most of the information in the next two sections comes from FedEx and Google's submission to CDP, as companies must respond to a set of questions detailing their "processes for identifying, assessing, and responding to climate-related risks and opportunities."[130]

FedEx

FedEx's current process for so identifying and responding to climate risks is incorporated into its overall risk assessment and management process, known as the Enterprise Risk Management (ERM) system. Consequently, climate risks and projects are treated the same as other types of risk in the company; investment decisions related to building climate resilience are integrated into decisionmaking processes for all of FedEx.[131] In terms of positions responsible for incorporating climate considerations into the ERM process, FedEx has a chief sustainability officer (CSO) who is responsible for assessing and managing climate-related risks and opportunities. The CSO meets at least annually with the Nominating and Governance Committee of FedEx's Board of Directors, which aids the board in overseeing corporate social responsibility initiatives, including matters related to climate change.[132]

FedEx's ERM process uses a consultative approach to determine risks to the company's operations, including those from climate change. Taking an enterprise approach, FedEx solicits input from the leaders of its operating companies on what they think are the company's biggest risks. Leaders identify risks in five main categories: external, strategic, operational, financial, and compliance. To ensure representation from across the company, FedEx uses three different methods for soliciting input. It conducts industry research on relevant risks, issues surveys to solicit input from company employees, and conducts workshops to further delve into potential risks.[133] The research and surveys inform the discussions held during the workshops, which focus on both identified and emerging risks. Once a list of risks is created, FedEx prioritizes

---

[130] Carbon Disclosure Project Worldwide, *FedEx Corporation—Climate Change 2021*, July 2021, p. 5; *Alphabet CDP Climate Change Response 2021*, Climate Disclosure Project, July 2021, p. 7.

[131] Carbon Disclosure Project Worldwide, 2021, pp. 4–5.

[132] Carbon Disclosure Project Worldwide, 2021, p. 2.

[133] The industry research informs the questions that are asked in the surveys.

them based on three factors: (1) likely financial impact, (2) probability of occurrence over the next year, and (3) level of current controls to manage the identified risk. Survey and workshop participants rank each risk on a scale of 1 to 5, resulting in an initial ranking of top enterprise risks. Each year, FedEx convenes a Risk Committee to review the initial risk ranking, which analyzes the initial set of responses and compiles a final list of top risks.[134]

Once the Risk Committee finalizes the list of identified risks, those given highest priority are shared with the company's Board of Trustees and Audit Committee. The committee also shares any potential significant changes across the entire list of risks with the board and Audit Committee. The top identified risks, including any of those related to climate change, serve as inputs into FedEx's capital investment processes. The Board of Directors decides which investments to make and take identified climate risks from the ERM process into consideration when making those decisions. The board allocates capital across the FedEx enterprise, including all operating companies. Investment decisions ultimately come down to needs and acceptable investment returns. Factoring in the identified climate risks, the board determines the amount and distribution of capital investments for specific items, such as aircraft and vehicle fleet modernization. FedEx provided examples of projects funded through this process that were intended to address climate change concerns. For instance, FedEx started its aircraft modernization program in 2013 and continues to fund the program to replace less–fuel-efficient aircraft with more-efficient models. FedEx also recently invested in a program to modernize its parcel pickup and delivery vehicle fleet. The goal of this program is to make all these vehicles zero-emission vehicles by 2040.[135]

Google

Similar to FedEx, Google incorporates its assessment of climate risks and opportunities, and the projects that address these, into its standard business risk assessment processes. Google's organization includes a sustainability board and a Google sustainability officer (GSO) position,[136] both of which focus on building the company's sustainability impact. The GSO reports to the board, providing information and updates on sustainability topics, including discussions of climate change risks. This information is also presented to the audit and compliance committee within Alphabet's board of directors.[137] The GSO may raise climate-related issues to the board at any time. The board also addresses climate change issues on an as-needed basis. In addition to serving as the main representative for sustainability issues, the GSO leads a companywide sustainability team. Members of this team represent different departments

---

[134] Carbon Disclosure Project Worldwide, 2021, p. 5.

[135] Carbon Disclosure Project Worldwide, 2021, p. 13.

[136] A GSO has primary responsibility for managing climate-related issues and reports to the company's chief financial officer. See *Alphabet CDP Climate Change Response*, 2021, p. 3.

[137] Alphabet is Google's parent company and is the company that submitted the report to CDP on behalf of Google.

from across the company, including those addressing real estate sustainability, data center sustainability, and consumer hardware sustainability. The sustainability team assists the GSO in developing sustainability targets and goals for the company, including those in financial management (and, thus, investment decisionmaking). The senior vice president and chief financial officer of Alphabet and Google provide senior leadership oversight on climate-related topics.[138]

According to its CDP submission, Google appears to assess climate risks and projects to address those risks in various levels and facets of the company. At the company level, the GSO works with risk management and operations teams to identify and assess climate risks and opportunities to mitigate and adapt to those risks. This process focuses on the risks and projects in the geographical areas where Google has the most infrastructure.[139] The climate risks and opportunities for these areas are assessed through models that employ such data as likely energy cost scenarios under different climate change regulations. The scenarios are then applied to estimate the potential costs to the company. The projects are also assessed in terms of how they will aid Google in meeting its goal of operating on carbon-free energy (CFE). At the physical, asset level, Google develops models to identify and assess relevant climate risks to physical sites. Google provided an example of such processes in its global office locations. For these entities, risks and opportunities are evaluated based on their specific geographical climate risk factors— that is, risks likely to occur in a given location. Google then applies three criteria to prioritize the risks and opportunities: (1) potential impact on its financial bottom line, (2) potential impact on its reputation, and (3) potential contribution to Google's goals of attaining 24/7 CFE and meeting GHG emissions targets. Each of these criteria is applied to each potential project, which are evaluated on a case-by-case basis. Google provided examples of the types of projects that this process has produced. For instance, Google improved the ecological system surrounding its Bay Area headquarters in California by planting native vegetation, adding riparian habitat, and planting 1,800 trees as a response to the identified risks posed by climate in the area.[140]

Google's CDP report states that clean energy projects are evaluated at the company level and contribute to its 24/7 CFE goal. Google detailed its 24/7 CFE initiative in a 2021 report to describe its approach to meeting this goal so that other organizations may learn from these efforts. Part of the report describes the process that Google uses to select clean energy projects

---

[138] *Alphabet CDP Climate Change Response*, 2021 p. 4.

[139] These areas are Google's headquarters in California's Bay Area, major global offices, and 23 data center locations. The risks and opportunities identified through this modeling process are reported to a cross-company and - functional group of stakeholders, which includes representatives from operations and finance. The results are also presented to the chief financial officer of Alphabet and Google, who can present that information to the Board of Directors whenever needed. Ultimately, senior leadership makes the final decisions on which projects or opportunities will be implemented to address the company's climate risks. *Alphabet CDP Climate Change Response*, 2021, p. 7.

[140] *Alphabet CDP Climate Change Response*, 2021, p. 7.

and how the company prioritizes different options.[141] Although these projects minimize the company's potential exposure to energy outages because of future climate change and/or climate-related regulations, they do not target the types of infrastructure resilience projects on which we focus in our proposed framework.[142] However, Google's process for prioritizing and selecting clean energy projects was one of the clearest we found outlined in our comparison case research and, thus, presented an example worthy of review. The following process outlines how Google considers and selects projects *within* a clean energy portfolio. From the report, it does not appear as though these are compared with other climate-related projects.[143]

Google's process for evaluating, prioritizing, and selecting clean energy projects can be boiled down to three primary steps:

1. Assess the project.
2. Evaluate how the project fits into Google's clean energy portfolio.
3. Determine a project's priority relative to other projects.[144]

Google assesses the value of proposed projects through two main metrics in relation to the costs of the project. The first metric, which measures the spend efficiency per percentage increase in the CFE score, reflects how the project will improve its CFE score. A lower score on this metric means that Google can reach higher levels of CFE at lower costs. The second metric assesses how the project will improve Google's avoided GHG emissions. This metric measures the spend efficiency of a project in terms of the amount of GHG emissions avoided. The lower the score on this metric, the better, because it indicates a higher level of emissions avoided at a lower cost.[145] Google calculates these metrics across a specific year or range of years and assesses these metrics at every potential transaction. The intent of applying the metrics across time and transactions is to assist Google in *right-sizing* projects—it helps them to ensure that it is not producing more CFE than its required load and, therefore, not spending more than needed on clean energy projects.[146]

With the above assessment completed and metric information in hand, Google uses an evaluation matrix to plot projects for comparison. The matrix assists in determining which projects should receive priority. The two-by-two matrix compares projects across the CFE and GHG emissions metrics. The matrix identifies which projects provide higher value across their

---

[141] *Alphabet CDP Climate Change Response*, 2021, p. 1.

[142] This process reflects the limitation we noted in the above section on how we selected our comparison cases and conducted research for this section. Although the processes we discuss do not focus exclusively on adapting to climate hazards, they still provide useful insights for how organizations are thinking about and developing processes to address climate challenges within their particular context.

[143] Google, *24/7 Carbon-Free Energy: Methodologies and Metrics*, February 2021.

[144] Google, 2021, p. 14.

[145] Google, 2021, pp. 14–15.

[146] Google, 2021, p. 15.

two metrics for their respective costs.[147] Google notes that although this project assessment and prioritization process is applied as its main guide for making investment decisions, it applies an additional set of factors when making its final decisions. These include regional constraints, long-term strategic investment, sustainability, and equity. Consequently, Google notes that it anticipates selecting projects from all four quadrants of its comparison matrix to meet the company's unique needs across geographical regions and time.[148]

Organizations' Approaches to Climate Uncertainty

As part of the research conducted for this chapter, we examined how the comparison organizations considered climate uncertainty in their project prioritization and investment-making processes. Although we reviewed all comparison organizations, we found the most-relevant and -robust information related to climate uncertainty in Army and NPS documentation. From this review, we discovered that they implement similar approaches, which we briefly highlight below.

Both the Army and NPS specifically incorporate climate uncertainty considerations in their infrastructure project planning processes, which feed into their project evaluation and selection processes. The Army directs planners to include uncertainty considerations in the second step of its four-step planning process, which aims to determine the "observed and expected future climate exposure themes" for an installation.[149] The second step includes two substeps, the first of which instructs planners to examine historical and current conditions to understand the types of hazards that the installation faced in the past and continues to encounter. The second substep instructs planners to identify and understand potential future hazards posed by climate change through the application and analysis of potential scenarios.[150] The NPS also applies climate scenarios during the second step of its four-step planning process, which instructs planners to identify climate futures and then assess climate vulnerabilities and risks.[151] NPS's method for developing climate futures includes distinguishing key climate threats and drivers for specific units. These factors should consider direct, indirect, and compounding (i.e., threat multiplier) effects. Taking this information, planners then develop two or more climate futures for a park

---

[147] Google, 2021, p. 15.

[148] Google, 2021, p. 16.

[149] Pinson et al., 2020, p. 29.

[150] Pinson et al., 2020, pp. 29, 39.

[151] Note that this planning process precedes the project prioritization processes described in the NPS section above. NPS planners assess the vulnerabilities of specific units under each potential future scenario. Planners then apply an assessment vulnerability framework to calculate the degree of exposure, the sensitivity of the resource, and the resource's adaptive capacity. They then summarize the impacts under each scenario and identify the highest risks to achieving desired outcomes. NPS, *Planning for a Changing Climate: Climate-Smart Planning and Management in the National Park Service*, 2021, p. 29.

unit. The NPS's main planning document on climate change, *Planning for a Changing Climate*, then instructs planners to organize climate hazards by their relative degrees of uncertainty.[152]

Both organizations employ multiple climate scenarios to address climate uncertainty. Army planners must identify potential climate hazards for both the *near future* of 2050 and *far future* of 2085. The *Army Climate Resilience Handbook* directs planners to apply different potential future scenarios to capture the variety of possible future conditions. By applying multiple scenarios, projects will encapsulate a wider set of potentialities.[153] Meanwhile, NPS encourages unit planners to avoid trying to forecast one particular scenario and avoid taking the mean of a set of climate models.[154] In *Planning for a Changing Climate*, NPS instructs unit planners to employ all potential outcomes for all projections and take these into account as equally as possible.[155] Essentially, as we heard in our discussion with NPS officials, thinking ahead and using multiple scenarios allow entities to develop and implement robust solutions that are responsive to multiple future scenarios, providing the flexibility needed to meet the uncertainty of the future.[156]

Organization Comparison: Findings and Considerations for the Air Force

Using our research on other organizations' approaches to incorporating climate change into their infrastructure investment processes, we identified common elements and practices that may be applied by other organizations seeking to develop and improve their own processes. The elements represent what we found to be common aspects of the decisionmaking processes, and the practices represent how those processes are implemented.

From our review of other organizations' investment-making processes, we developed the following process map to capture common elements. Not all organizations included every element in their individual process; we included an element if at least two of the five organizations applied it in their process. The process map, therefore, presents a general illustration of how organizations incorporate climate change considerations into their investment decisionmaking (Figure 4.1).

---

[152] The NPS uses the term *climate driver*, rather than *climate hazard*, to describe "any climate-related factors (e.g., temperature, precipitation, sea level) that directly or indirectly affect, or have the potential to affect, a park's resources and assets" (NPS, 2021, pp. 27–30).

[153] Pinson et al., 2020, pp. 16, 39.

[154] NPS official, interview with authors, June 3, 2022; NPS, 2021, p. 26.

[155] NPS, 2020, p. 31.

[156] NPS official, interview with authors, June 3, 2022.

Figure 4.1. Common Elements of Climate Resilience Project Prioritization and Selection Processes

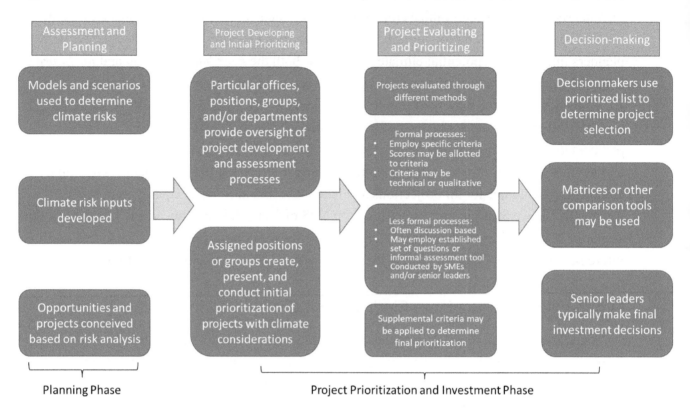

In addition to identifying and visualizing a generalized common process, our research illuminated several common and notable practices for integrating climate factors into investment decisions. Some of these practices reflect the common elements of the general process illustrated in this figure, but at a broader level. The common practices among our comparison organizations include the following:

- All organizations incorporated, or are working to incorporate, climate change resilience factors into their existing risk assessment and investment-making decision processes.
- All organizations make decisions to invest in projects that boost climate resilience based on the project's ability to meet the entity's mission or submission.
- All organizations' processes include senior leadership consultation and involvement, often occurring in the review and/or final decision approval phases.
- At least three of the reviewed organizations solicited input from across the organization for ideas on how to address climate risks.
- All organizations developed and applied sets of criteria to evaluate the impact of climate resilience factors in proposed projects. Most organizations applied different types of criteria to capture both technical and qualitative factors.
- At least two organizations developed or are developing specialized project portfolios to address specific elements of climate resilience.

In addition to common practices, our research uncovered the following notable practices implemented by individual organizations:

- The NPS created a working lexicon of climate-related terms to ensure consistent understanding and application of climate concepts in its plans and processes.
- The NPS is developing processes for sharing relevant climate information across the agency to assist park unit staff in their climate risk assessments and senior-level managers in their decisionmaking efforts.
- Google is publicly sharing information on its processes to encourage and assist other companies to take steps to address climate change.

Applying Common Practices Through Our Proposed Framework

The Air Force may consider incorporating any of the common or notable practices identified above into its current or future project prioritization and investment processes. To provide a sense of how this might be done, we considered how the six common practices listed above could be applied through the assessment framework presented in Chapter 3. Table 4.2 shows how the framework already aligns with, or may incorporate, some of the common practices, depending on how the Air Force applies the framework.

Table 4.2. Applying Common Practices Through Proposed Framework

Common Practice	Application of Practice Through Proposed Framework
Organizations incorporated, or are working to incorporate, climate change resilience factors into their existing risk assessment and investment-making decision processes.	The framework may be applied in multiple existing Air Force processes. For example, AFCEC may apply the framework during its assessment of projects for FSRM funding. The framework could also be applied by the MILCON working group to assist in making military construction funding decisions.
Organizations make decisions to invest in climate resilience projects based on the project's ability to meet the entity's mission or submission.	The framework includes a mission-oriented measure (TMDI or similar) to ensure that proposed projects support an installation's mission.
Organizations' processes include senior leadership consultation and involvement, often in review and/or final decision approval phases.	Depending on where the Air Force applies the framework in its existing processes, senior leaders may use the tool as part of their decisionmaking efforts.
Organizations solicited input from across the organization for ideas on how to address climate risks.	The framework requires input on climate risks and potential projects from across installations.
Organizations developed and incorporated sets of criteria to evaluate the impact of climate resilience factors in proposed projects.	The framework provides the criteria that the Air Force can use to assess the impact of climate resilience factors in proposed projects.
Organizations developed or are developing specialized project portfolios to address specific elements of climate resilience.	The DAF may use the framework to help determine whether specialized portfolios should be established.

Although this research task focused on identifying our specific comparison organizations' processes for incorporating climate change into their infrastructure investment-making decisions, we also conducted a high-level, targeted search for literature related to this topic. In doing so, we hoped to compare what, if any, practices the literature recommended with those we identified in our comparison cases. Our search led to few relevant sources. As organizations begin to develop and implement their processes, it makes sense that little research has yet to be done to identify best practices for incorporating climate change into infrastructure investments at the national level. However, one recent U.S. Government Accountability Office (GAO) report addressed the topic of how federal agencies could identify and implement projects to address climate resilience.[157] In the report, GAO notes that the federal government has yet to develop its own strategic approach to identifying and prioritizing climate resilience projects for investment. To help the federal government in doing so, GAO recommended six key steps, from defining the project's goals to monitoring the project once implemented. Some parts of the recommended steps, including designating particular entities to oversee project development and assessment, using models and scenarios to determine climate risks and evaluate projects, and using criteria to assess which projects should be implemented first, aligned with process elements presented in Figure 4.1.[158] In the fourth step of prioritizing projects, GAO made recommendations that were related to common practices we identified, including soliciting input from a wide variety of stakeholders and employing different sets of criteria to prioritize projects.[159] Thus, initial research, although limited, supported multiple aspects of our comparison cases' processes.

Our examination of comparison organizations revealed that other entities are still developing processes to incorporate climate change into their infrastructure investment-making decisions. By reviewing their progress thus far, we were able to identify common elements of those processes and practices that support the implementation of those processes. These practices could be carried out by the DAF through the implementation of our proposed framework in Chapter 3 and through supporting elements as the DAF builds and refines its investment-making processes.

---

[157] GAO, *Climate Resilience: A Strategic Investment Approach for High-Priority Projects Could Help Target Federal Resources*, October 23, 2019.

[158] GAO, 2019, pp. 29, 31–34, 38–42.

[159] GAO, 2019, pp. 37–42.

Chapter 5. Key Findings and Recommendations

In this concluding chapter, we summarize key findings from our research, identify data and information needs related to framework implementation, and recommend next steps for the DAF, should it choose to implement the framework.

Summary of Key Findings

- The review of DAF documents described in Chapter 2 provided detailed and grounded understanding of current policy and guidance regarding resilience, clarifying the roles of organizations that lead climate-related efforts relevant to installations. Additional review of resilience definitions and existing frameworks (e.g., RDVM) provided a basis for the structure of our framework.
- Interviews with key DAF stakeholders and SMEs confirmed the need for a systematic framework for comparing and prioritizing projects based on their climate resilience value.
- Our review of other organizations' approaches to climate resilience investment decisionmaking revealed common practices and process elements, which largely align with key components of our proposed framework and further support the potential efficacy of such an approach. Similar to the DAF, our comparison federal agencies are primarily in the development and evaluation phases for their climate risk assessment processes, while private-sector comparisons have incorporated climate into their ESG considerations in their standard risk management processes.
- Climate uncertainty presents a key challenge for resilience planning and, therefore, should play a role in any approach taken to setting resilience investment priorities. In Chapter 3, we offered suggestions for how to account for this uncertainty in the framework's implementation.

Requisite Data and Models

We used several data sources to illustrate the framework presented in Chapter 3. We summarize these sources in Table 5.1. The DAF will need to use these or analogous sources to build the dataset necessary to implement the framework. Much of the data preparation required to carry out Steps 1 and 3 of the framework (characterizing baseline asset exposure and describing projects' exposure reduction potential) could be done in advance and centrally, thereby limiting the amount of data collection or analysis that installations must do each time a project is submitted for consideration. Chapter 3 and Appendix C describe in detail the steps we took to compile requisite data and turn them into usable inputs for the framework.

Table 5.1. Summary of Data Sources Used to Populate Framework

Source	Readily Usable?	If Not Readily Usable, What Steps Are Needed to Make the Data Usable?	Notes
GeoBase (asset locations and numbers)	Yes	N/A	Most reliably available for buildings rather than point-based assets
RPAD (PRV)	Yes	N/A	Does not include value of contents within buildings (e.g., equipment)
TMDI	Yes/no	TMDI values may be readily associated with GeoBase assets, but requires squadron attributes to be standardized to crosswalk with other datasets (e.g., RPAD, DRRS-S)	N/A
DRRS-S (unit types for uniqueness analysis)	No	Requires unit types to be mapped to squadron types (TMDI)	RAND generated a mapping of unit types to squadron types for notional projects included in analysis
SWP worksheets (self-reported hazard exposure)	No	Requires aggregating individual worksheets	N/A
DCAT (flood exposure)	Yes	N/A	May overestimate flood extents and does not differentiate levels of exposure by flood depth
FlamMap outputs (wildfire exposure)	No	Requires assessment of local weather conditions	Requires subjective selection of a burn probability threshold

Step 2 of the framework (defining a benefiting area) requires localized expertise and judgment related to the realm of influence of the project in question. Step 4 primarily hinges on decisionmaker judgment and preferences, particularly when it comes to assigning weight to the different metrics used to compare projects.

Recommendations for Implementing the Framework

We offer several recommendations related to ensuring that the framework is situated in current DAF processes in a way that serves those who stand to benefit from it most, that data needed to populate the framework are made available to those who might be asked to implement it, and that climate uncertainty is not overlooked.

Identify specific steps in existing or anticipated project planning, prioritization, and validation processes in which such a framework would be most useful. The proposed framework could be used to support several DAF processes and activities such as the following:

- *Requirements identification and project submission.* Installations routinely seek funding for projects, and regardless of the specific process or funding stream (e.g., centralized FSRM or MILCON) to which the request is tied, installations need to be able to articulate the value of a given project. To the extent that climate resilience is or becomes a lens through which projects are evaluated and prioritized, completing Steps 1–3 of the framework presented in this report can help organizations communicate their installations' relative resilience benefits afforded by a project in a data-informed, standardized way, for example, by comparing standardized metrics, such as numbers of benefiting assets and PRV (see, e.g., Tables 3.7 and 3.8).

- *Project prioritization.* Whether at the installation level (e.g., Facilities Board prioritization of MILCON project presubmissions) or at the MAJCOM level (e.g., when assigning priority points), those responsible for prioritizing projects would benefit from having a way to compare projects based on their climate resilience–enhancing potential while acknowledging that these resilience benefits must be assessed in the context of the broader value that such projects offer to the enterprise as a whole.
- *Review and validation of projects by AFCEC/AFIMSC.* Outputs of the first three steps of the framework can serve as a concrete basis for AFCEC/AFIMSC's engagements with installations, MAJCOMs, or AFIMSC detachments as part of project validation.
- *Development of ICRPs.* As installations and AFCEC work together to develop these plans, having a systematic way to highlight the climate resilience value of projects can help organizations respond to congressional or other requests for justifications of project selection.

Ultimately, the decision of where in current processes and by whom the framework is used should follow from a deeper understanding of the need for the framework and capacity for uptake in different contexts. Socializing the idea and seeking feedback from potential users should be first steps in operationalizing the framework.

Identify project pools in which the framework might be applied. For instance, the framework could be applied to just a subset of projects with comparable (high) costs or only to those projects tagged as having resilience value in the MILCON IPL tool (discussed in Chapter 2). Limiting the framework's application in this way can help to reduce the administrative burden placed on installations (by not requiring that *all* projects be subjected to a systematic evaluation of their climate resilience potential).

Another way to confine the set of projects to which the framework is applied is by including just those projects in the pool that are similar (e.g., in terms of costs or programmatic risks) *except* for their potential to enhance climate resilience. For such projects, the most useful dimension for comparison is their relative effectiveness at reducing exposure to hazards of interest, which the framework is designed to support.

Compile, adapt, or generate data and information elements needed to apply the framework and identify appropriate entities for carrying out each step. Much of the data requisite for completing Steps 1 and 3 of the framework can be generated centrally (e.g., by AFCEC) and in advance of applying the framework (i.e., Step 0). For instance, characterizing the baseline exposure of installation assets does not require knowledge of specific projects and can be completed in advance by analysts with access to the types of centralized datasets that we describe throughout this report. Then, for installations, Step 1 becomes a relatively simple matter of pulling relevant information from a central dataset rather than having to generate new information from scratch for each new project submission.

Unlike in Step 1, the information needed to complete Step 2 cannot be compiled ahead of time due its shift in focus to specific projects. Installation personnel will need to use their local knowledge to define the benefiting area for each project.

Step 3 assesses the anticipated effect of a project on reducing exposure to some hazard and, therefore, cannot be completed ahead of time, outside the context of a specific project. That said, with a clear definition of an exposed asset in Step 1 and a well-defined process for deciding whether an asset falls within the benefiting area in Step 2, this step is relatively straightforward to complete.

Finally, Step 4 relies on decisionmaker (e.g., MAJCOM leadership) judgment to select preferred projects. Decisionmakers will need to weight the different metrics considered in Steps 1 and 3 as they choose preferred projects for their particular mission(s). For instance, different levels of exposure reduction might be desirable for different missions. There is no substitute for the use of judgment in completing this final step of the framework. Depending on the extent of a decisionmaker's familiarity with mission needs and the relative importance of reducing exposure to different missions of interest, additional data beyond what supported Steps 1–3 might not be needed to complete this step.

Create concrete methods to inject relevant data into current processes. For instance, centrally generated information in Step 0 could be integrated into planning platforms or portals that AFCEC and/or the Comprehensive Planning Division (CPP) maintains, which would help to expedite the exposure analysis of Step 1. Similarly, a new block in Form 1391 (or space in advocacy slides that accompany project submissions) could be added specifically for installations to define the "benefiting area" of projects, which could greatly streamline and simplify the required analysis in Step 2.[160]

Account for climate uncertainty throughout. Those implementing the framework should consider multiple climate scenarios in estimations of baseline exposure (in Step 1) and exposure reductions (in Step 3) and consider whether multiple climate scenarios could inform selection of the appropriate benefiting area for a project (Step 2). In Step 4, robust and adaptive strategies should be favored over those optimized only for present conditions.

Climate-related hazards have long posed a threat to DAF installations, and the threat is here to stay. As the DAF continues to understand the effects of these hazards on installations and their missions, it will increasingly need to make tough choices about where and how much to invest in boosting installation and mission resilience. Having a structured approach to guide infrastructure

---

[160] DD Form 1391 is used by DoD "to submit documented requirements necessary for the submittal of program justification in support of funding requests for military construction projects" (U.S. Army Corps of Engineers, "DD1391 Processor System," fact sheet, updated July 28, 2022).

investments decisionmaking, like the one presented in this report, can help ensure that scarce resources are efficiently allocated to address the biggest mission risks most effectively.

Appendix A. Document Review and Resilience Definitions

This appendix presents all documents included in the literature review as described in Chapter 2 (see the Document Review section), definitions of resilience obtained from the resilience literature and resilience-related definitions from the DAF and DoD (see the "Definitions and Concepts of Resilience" section), results from a detailed review of DAF facilities standards (see the "Review of Facilities Standards" section), and RAND reports reviewed in support of comparison organization selection in Chapter 4 (see the "Organizational Comparison Documents" section).

Document Review

Table A.1 lists the DAF and DoD documents that we reviewed.

Table A.1. DAF and DoD Documents Reviewed

Document	Department	Year	Document Type
AFDP 3-59, *Weather Operations*	DAF	2020	Policy
Air Force Installation Energy Plans	DAF	2021	Fact sheet
AFI 32-1015, *Integrated Installation Planning*	DAF	2021	Policy
AFI 32-7020, *Environmental Restoration Program*, Department of the Air Force, March 2020	DAF	2020	Policy
AFI 32-7091, *Environmental Management Outside the United States*, Department of the Air Force, November 2019	DAF	2019	Policy
AFI 90-802, *Risk Management*, Department of the Air Force, April 1, 2019	DAF	2019	Policy
AFI 90-1701, *Installation Energy and Water Management*, Department of the Air Force, April 1, 2019	DAF	2020	Policy
AFI 90-2001, *Mission Sustainment*	DAF	2019	Policy
Air Force Manual 15-129, *Air and Space Weather Operations*, Department of the Air Force, July 2020	DAF	2020	Policy
Air Force Manual 32-7003, *Environmental Conservation*, Department of the Air Force, April 2020	DAF	2020	Policy
AFPD 32-10, *Installations and Facilities*, Department of the Air Force, July 2020	DAF	2020	Policy
AFPD 32-70, *Environmental Considerations in Air Force Programs and Activities*, Department of the Air Force, July 2018	DAF	2018	Policy
AFPD 90-17, *Energy and Water Management*, Department of the Air Force, May 2020	DAF	2020	Policy
AFPD 90-20, *Mission Sustainment*	DAF	2019	Policy
Center for Climate and Security, *Background Paper on Top 10 Air Force Bases at Risk of Weather Impacts*, undated	DAF	2019	Policy
Comprehensive Planning Chronicle	DAF	2021	Article
Mark Correll, "Where Mission Assurance Meets Energy Assurance," *Military Engineer*, Vol. 113, No. 72, March–April 2021	DAF	2021	Article
Crown Jewels Analysis	DAF	2021	Fact sheet
Department of the Air Force, *Installation Energy Strategic Plan*, U.S. Department of Defense, 2021	DAF	2021	Strategic plan
DoDD 3020.40, *Mission Assurance*	DoD	2018	Policy
DoDD 4715.21, *Climate Change Adaptation and Resilience*	DoD	2016	Policy
DoDI 3200.21, *Sustaining Access to the Live Training Domain*	DoD	2020	Policy

Document	Department	Year	Document Type
Energy Resilience Readiness Exercise	DAF	2021	Fact sheet
Energy-as-a-Service	DAF	2021	Fact sheet
Facility Engineering Directorate	AFCEC	2017	Fact sheet
Christina Hudson and Greg Hammer, *Addressing Severe Weather and Climate Threats at Installations from a Planning Perspective*, Air Force Installation and Mission Support Center, May 2021.	DAF	2021	Article
ICRP	DAF	N/A	Strategic plan
IDP	DAF	N/A	Strategic plan
Installation Energy Program Overview	DAF	2021	Fact sheet
Installations Directorate	AFCEC	2018	Fact sheet
Installation Water Dashboard	DAF	2021	Fact sheet
Micro-Reactor Pilot Program	DAF	2021	Fact sheet
Mission Thread Analysis	DAF	2021	Fact sheet
Office of the Deputy Assistant Secretary for Environment, Safety, and Infrastructure, *Micro-Reactor Pilot FAQs*, Department of the Air Force, October 27, 2021.	DAF	2021	Fact sheet
Office of the Undersecretary for Policy for Strategy, Plans, and Capabilities, *Department of Defense Climate Risk Analysis*, U.S. Department of Defense, October 2021.	DoD	2021	Policy
Planning and Integration Directorate	AFCEC	2017	Fact sheet
Readiness Directorate	AFCEC	2012	Fact sheet
Resilient Energy Savings Resources Vault	DAF	2020	Fact sheet
SWP	DAF	2020	Guidebook
Systems Modeling	DAF	2021	Fact sheet
UFC 1-200-02, *High Performance and Sustainable Building Requirements, with Change 2*, U.S. Department of Defense, December 1, 2020.	DoD	2020, 2022	UFC
UFC 2-100-1, *Installation Master Planning*	DoD	2020, 2022	UFC
UFC 3-201-01, *Civil Engineering*	DoD	2018, 2022	UFC
UFC 3-201-02, *Landscape Architecture*, U.S. Department of Defense, April 29, 2020, change 1, February 9, 2021.	DoD	2020	UFC
UFC 3-301-01, *Structural Engineering*, U.S. Department of Defense, April 11, 2023.	DoD	2019, 2022	UFC
UFC 3-400-02, *Design: Engineering Weather Data*, U.S. Department of Defense, September 20, 2018.	DoD	2018	UFC

Document	Department	Year	Document Type
U.S. Department of Defense, *Department of Defense Climate Adaptation Plan*, 2021.	DoD	2021	Strategic plan
U.S. Senate, Military Infrastructure and Climate Resilience: Hearing Before the Subcommittee on Military Construction, Veterans Affairs, and Related Agencies, May 19, 2021.	DAF	2021	Witness statement
Heather Wilson and David L. Goldfein, "United States Air Force Infrastructure Investment Strategy," memorandum for record, Department of the Air Force, January 29, 2019.	DAF	2019	Strategic plan
Water Resources Management	DAF	2021	Fact sheet

SOURCE: RAND compilation of DAF and DoD documents.

Definitions and Concepts of Resilience

We conducted a review of definitions and concepts related to resilience to define *climate resilience* in the context of our research. Resilience is commonly framed in terms of capacities of systems to function at various points before and after a stressing event. Acknowledging the dynamic nature of hazards, Norris et al. describes a disruption as a *stressor*, which may vary in severity, duration, and predictability; come as a surprise event, such as a fire or an earthquake; or represent an enduring stressor, such as flooding or extreme heat.[162] In terms of relevant system characteristics, Bhoite and colleagues outline elements of resilient systems in their 2015 *City Resilience Framework* as follows:

- Reflective: Systems should have mechanisms that continuously evolve.
- Robust: Systems should anticipate potential failures and make provisions to ensure that failure is not disproportionate to cause.
- Redundant: Systems should have spare capacity to accommodate disruption, pressure, and change.
- Flexible: Systems should be able to change, evolve, and adapt.
- Resourceful: People and institutions should be able to find different ways to achieve their goals.
- Inclusive: Systems should promote community engagement.
- Integrated: There should be alignment between systems should be pursued to promote consistency.[163]

Particularly relevant to the research presented in this report, frameworks detailing a system's elements can serve as tools to support decisionmaking. For example, the Absorptive, Restorative, Equitable Access and Adaptive (AREA) approach to resilience can help decisionmaking identify and understand these capacities of systems. Understanding the different capacities, and the parts of the system that contribute to those capacities, provides alternatives to investment strategies[164] or possible trade-offs in investment that can be made to determine which projects should be prioritized. The AREA approach focuses on the ability to (1) maintain a functioning system while considering assets' capacities to absorb stresses and restore services quickly, (2) ensure equitable access to essential assets and services in a community or installation, and (3) ensure that the system can adapt by changing a response. Also, it is important to understand that capacity of systems likely relies on interdependencies across systems or infrastructure. As

---

[162] Norris et al., 2008, p. 131.

[163] Sachin Bhoite, Kieran Birtill, Stephen Cook, Sandra Diaz, Vicky Evans, Andrea Fernandez, Laura Frost, Sam Kernaghan, Ashlee Loiacono, Braulio Eduardo Morera, Geoffrey Morgan, Elizabeth Parker, Jo da Silva, Samantha Stratton-Short, and Flora Tonking, *City Resilience Framework*, Arup International Development, updated December 2015.

[164] Sarah Weilant, Aaron Strong, and Benjamin M. Miller, *Incorporating Resilience into Transportation Planning and Assessment*, RAND Corporation, RR-3038-TRB, 2019, pp. 24–25.

Bruneau et al. (2003) highlights, certain assets or infrastructure are needed for certain services—for example, power is needed for water delivery[165]—and an understanding of these interdependencies depends on the ability to define, measure, and articulate impacts or benefits of parts of the system.[166]

A comprehensive list of resilience definitions from resilience literature, obtained from a paraphrasing of Norris et al. in a previous RAND study is presented in Table A.2.[167] Definitions of resilience found in policy documents described in Chapter 2 are shown in Table A.3. According to our review of the following definitions and our understanding of elements of resilience systems presented above, for the purposes of this study, *climate resilience* can be understood as the capacity of a system to absorb, adapt to, and recover from or restore functioning in the event of a climate-related stressor.

Table A.2. Sample Definitions of Resilience in Analysis

Source	Level of Analysis	Paraphrased Definition
Resilience Alliance, "Key Concepts," webpage, undated	Ecological system	The capacity of a system to absorb disturbance and reorganize while undergoing change so as to retain essentially the same function, structure, and feedbacks—and therefore the same identity
C. S. Holling, "Resilience and Stability of Ecological Systems," *Annual Review of Ecology and Systematics*, Vol. 4, No. 1, 1973	Ecological system	The persistence of relationships within a system; a measure of the ability of systems to absorb changes of state variables, driving variables, and parameters and still persist
J. E. Gordon, *Structures*, Penguin Books, 1978	Physical	The ability to store strain energy and deflect elastically under a load without breaking or being deformed
Ann S. Masten, Karin M. Best, and Norman Garmezy, "Resilience and Development: Contributions from the Study of Children Who Overcome Adversity," *Development and Psychopathology*, Vol. 2, No. 4, October 1990	Individual	The process of, capacity for, or outcome of successful adaptation despite challenging or threatening circumstances
Byron Egeland, Elizabeth Carlson, and L. Alan Sroufe, "Resilience as Process," *Development and*	Individual	The capacity for successful adaptation, positive functioning, or competence despite high-risk status or chronic stress, or following prolonged or severe trauma

---

[165] Bruneau et al., 2003.

[166] For more historical framing on resilience and capacity, see Adam Rose, "Defining and Measuring Economic Resilience to Disasters," *Disaster Prevention and Management*, Vol. 13, No. 4, 2004; and Royce Francis and Behailu Bekera, "A Metric and Frameworks for Resilience Analysis of Engineered and Infrastructure Systems," *Reliability Engineering & System Safety*, Vol. 121, January 2014.

[167] Weilant, Strong, and Miller, 2019.

Source	Level of Analysis	Paraphrased Definition
Psychopathology, Vol. 5, No. 4, October 1993		
David D. Brown and Judith Celene Kulig, "The Concepts of Resiliency: Theoretical Lessons from Community Research," *Health and Canadian Society*, Vol. 4, No. 1, 1996–1997	Community	The ability to recover from or adjust easily to misfortune or sustained life stress
Christopher C. Fisher "Sense of Community: Community Resilient Responses to Oppression and Change," *Journal of Community Psychology*, Vol. 26, No. 5, 1998	Community	The process through which mediating structures (schools, peer groups, and family) and activity settings moderate the impact of oppressive systems
W. Neil Adger, "Social and Ecological Resilience: Are They Related?" *Progress in Human Geography*, Vol. 24, No. 3, 2000	Social	The ability of communities to withstand external shocks to their social infrastructure
Paton and Johnston, 2000	Community	The capability to bounce back and to use physical and economic resources effectively to aid recovery following exposure to hazards
Bruneau et al., 2003	Social	The ability of social units to mitigate hazards, contain the effects of disasters when they occur, and carry out recovery activities in ways that minimize social disruption and mitigate the effects of future earthquakes
Ganor and Ben-Levy, 2003	Community	The ability of individuals and communities to deal with a state of continuous, long-term stress; the ability to find unknown inner strengths and resources to cope effectively; the measure of adaptation and flexibility
David R. Godschalk, "Urban Hazard Mitigation: Creating Resilient Cities," *Natural Hazards Review*, Vol. 4, No. 3, August 2003	City	A sustainable network of physical systems and human communities capable of managing extreme events; during disaster, both must be able to survive and function under extreme stress
Richard J. T. Klein, Robert J. Nicholls, and Frank Thomalla, "Resilience to Natural Hazards: How Useful Is This Concept?" *Global Environmental Change*, Part B: *Environmental Hazards*, Vol. 5, Nos. 1–2, 2003	Ecological system	The ability of a system that has undergone stress to recover and return to its original state; more precisely (1) the amount of disturbance a system can absorb and still remain within the same state or domain of attraction and (2) the degree to which the system is capable of self-organization (see also Steve Carpenter, Brian Walker, J. Marty Anderies, and Nick Abel, "From Metaphor to Measurement: Resilience of What to What?" *Ecosystems*, Vol. 4, 2001).
Rashid Ahmed, Mohamed Seedat, Ashley van Niekerk, and Samed Bulbulia, "Discerning Community Resilience in Disadvantaged Communities in the Context of Violence and Injury	Community	The development of material, physical, sociopolitical, sociocultural, and psychological resources that promote the safety of residents and buffer adversity

Source	Level of Analysis	Paraphrased Definition
Prevention," *South African Journal of Psychology*, Vol. 34, No. 3, 2004		
Per Bodin and Bo L. B. Wiman, "Resilience and Other Stability Concepts in Ecology: Notes on Their Origin, Validity, and Usefulness," *ESS Bulletin*, Vol. 2, No. 2, 2004	Physical	The speed with which a system returns to equilibrium after displacement, irrespective of how many oscillations are required
Eve Coles and Philip Buckle, "Developing Community Resilience as a Foundation for Effective Disaster Recovery," *Australian Journal of Emergency Management*, Vol. 19, No. 4, November 2004	Community	A community's capacities, skills, and knowledge that allow it to participate fully in recovery from disasters
Shaul Kimhi and Michal Shamai, "Community Resilience and the Impact of Stress: Adult Response to Israel's Withdrawal from Lebanon," *Journal of Community Psychology*, Vol. 32, No. 4, July 2004	Community	Individuals' sense of the ability of their own community to deal successfully with the ongoing political violence
Patricia H. Longstaff, *Security, Resilience, and Communication in Unpredictable Environments Such as Terrorism, Natural Disasters, and Complex Technology*, Center for Information Policy Research, Harvard University, November 2005	Ecological system	The ability by an individual, group, or organization to continue its existence (or remain more or less stable) in the face of some sort of surprise; resilience is found in systems that are highly adaptable (not locked into specific strategies) and have diverse resources
Betty J. Pfefferbaum, Dori B. Reissman, Rose L. Pfefferbaum, Richard W. Klomp, and Robin H. Gurwitch, "Building Resilience to Mass Trauma Events," in Lynda S. Doll, Sandra E. Bonzo, David A. Sleet, and James A. Mercy, eds., *Handbook of Injury and Violence Prevention*, Springer, 2006	Community	The ability of community members to take meaningful, deliberate, collective action to remedy the impact of a problem, including the ability to interpret the environment, intervene, and move on
Lisa D. Butler, Leslie A. Morland, and Gregory A. Leskin, "Psychological Resilience in the Face of Terrorism," in Bruce Bongar, Lisa M. Brown,	Individual	Good adaptation under extenuating circumstances; a recovery trajectory that returns to baseline functioning following a challenge

Source	Level of Analysis	Paraphrased Definition
Larry E. Beutler, James N. Breckenridge, and Philip G. Zimbardo, eds., *Psychology of Terrorism*, Oxford University Press, 2007		

Table A.3. DAF and DoD Definitions of Resilience or Related Factors

Document	Definition
AFI 32-1015	**Military installation resilience**—The capability of a military installation to avoid, prepare for, minimize the effect of, adapt to, and recover from extreme weather events, or from anticipated or unanticipated changes in environmental conditions, that do, or have the potential to, adversely affect the military installation or essential transportation, logistical, or other necessary resources outside the military installation that are necessary to maintain, improve, or rapidly reestablish installation mission assurance and mission-essential functions (p. 87). **Resilience**—The ability to anticipate, prepare for, and adapt to changing conditions and withstand, respond to, and recover rapidly from disruptions (p. 90). **Task critical asset**—An asset that is of such extraordinary importance that its incapacitation or destruction would have a serious, debilitating effect on the ability of one or more DoD or [Office of the Secretary of Defense] components to execute the capability or mission-essential task it supports. Task critical assets are used to identify defense critical assets (p. 91). **Integrated installation planning**—An integrated, interdisciplinary planning approach that combines all internal and external installation planning programs, processes, and products used to influence and guide the future physical development of Air Force installations. Integrated installation planning encompasses all aspects of installation asset management, encroachment, planning, and development covered by this instruction (p. 85). **Climate change**—Variations in average weather conditions that persist over multiple decades or longer, which encompass increases and decreases in temperature, shifts in precipitation, and changing risk of certain types of severe weather events (p. 80). **Hazard**—Any real or potential condition that can cause mission degradation, injury, illness, or death to personnel or damage to or loss of equipment or property (p. 83). **Severe weather**—Any weather condition that poses a hazard to property or life (p. 90).
DAF Installation Energy Strategic Plan	**The 5Rs:** (1) Robustness: incorporates the concept of reliability and refers to the ability to withstand disturbances; (2) Redundancy: having excess capacity and back-up systems, which enable the maintenance of core functionality in the event of disturbances; (3) Resourcefulness: ability to adapt to crises, respond flexibly, and neutralize negative impacts; (4) Response: ability to mobilize quickly in a crisis; and (5) Recovery: ability to regain a degree of normality after an event, be flexible, and evolve to deal with new circumstances (p. 8).
AFPD 90-17	**Energy resilience**—The ability to avoid, prepare for, minimize, adapt to, and recover from anticipated and unanticipated energy disruptions to ensure energy availability and reliability sufficient to provide for mission assurance and readiness, including mission-essential operations related to readiness, and to execute or rapidly reestablish mission-essential requirements (p. 6). **Water resilience**—The reliable ability to access an adequate quantity and quality of water to meet mission requirements while also mitigating water-related risks to mission success (p. 7).
AFI 90-1701	**Attributes of resilience**—The DAF should use the following three preventive attributes and two performance attributes to evaluate the resilience aspects of energy and water projects— conversationally referred to as *the 5Rs* (see "The 5Rs" above) (p. 19).
AFI 90-802	**Hazard**—A condition with the potential to cause injury, illness, or death of personnel; damage to or loss of equipment or property; or mission degradation (p. 29). **Knock-it-off/timeout concepts**—A safety call, using sound risk management, made by any participant during an activity or operation, immediately halting all actions until the situation is stabilized to a safe position (p. 29). **Real-time risk management**—A level of risk management that includes risk management decisions made in real-time, such as short-notice taskings, responding to emergency situations or making spur-of-the-moment decisions during tactical or training operations (p. 29).

Document	Definition
	Risk—The probability and severity of loss or adverse impact from exposure to various hazards (p. 29).
	Risk assessment—The process of detecting hazards and their causes and systematically assessing the associated risks (p. 30).
	Risk management—The systematic process of identifying hazards, assessing risk, making control decisions, implementing control decisions, and supervising and reviewing the activity for effectiveness (p. 30).
	Significant mishap or event—A Class A or B mishap or any other mishap or event deemed worthy of review by the organization's commander where lessons may be identified or learned for future application both inside and outside the organization (p. 30).
AFPD 90-20	**Control**—A deliberate action taken to reduce or eliminate the risk of a hazard(s) on Air Force activities, facilities, equipment, or personnel. Controls are most commonly initiated and monitored by the Installation Mission Sustainment Team. Effective controls reduce hazard probability, severity, or both (p. 7).
	Hazard—Any real or potential condition that can cause mission degradation, injury, illness, death to personnel, or damage to or loss of equipment or property (p. 8).
AFPD 32-10	**Risk**—Probability and severity of loss linked to hazards (p. 7).
AFI 90-2001	**Mission sustainment hazard categories: climate/weather**—Susceptibility to drought, flooding, wildland fires, ecosystem disruption, severe weather, or change in disease vectors (p. 19).
AFDP 3-59	**Weather**—The physical conditions of the terrestrial and space environment. These conditions include any environmental factors from the surface of the earth up to the ionosphere and outward into space (p.1).
Department of Defense Climate Risk Analysis	**Climate change**—Variations in average weather conditions that persist over multiple decades or longer, which encompass increases and decreases in temperature, shifts in precipitation, and changing risk of certain types of severe weather events. (DoDD 4715.21, Joint Publication (JP) 1-02, *Department of Defense Dictionary of Military and Associated Terms*, amended November 15, 2012) (p. 5)
	Hazard—A condition with the potential to cause injury, illness, or death of personnel; damage to or loss of equipment or property; or mission degradation. (JP 1-02, 2012) (p. 5)
	Resilience—The ability to anticipate, prepare for, and adapt to changing conditions and withstand, respond to, and recover rapidly from disruptions. (DoDD 4715.21) (p. 5)
Department of Defense Climate Adaptation Plan	**Adaptation**—Adjustment in natural or human systems in anticipation of or response to a changing environment in a way that effectively uses beneficial opportunities or reduces negative efforts (p. 2).
	Resilience—The ability to anticipate, prepare for, and adapt to changing conditions and withstand, respond to, and recover rapidly from disruptions (p. 2).
	Mitigation—Measures to reduce the amount and speed of future climate change by reducing emissions of heat-trapping gases or removing carbon dioxide from the atmosphere (p. 2).
JP 3-14, *Space Operations*, change 1, April 10, 2018, Joint Chiefs of Staff, October 26, 2020	**Resilience**—The ability of an architecture to support the functions necessary for mission success with higher probability; with shorter periods of reduced capability; and across a wider variety of scenarios, conditions, and threats, in spite of hostile action or adverse conditions. Resilience may leverage cross-domain or alternative government, commercial, or international capabilities. Unlike defensive operations and reconstitution, resilience is an internally focused characteristic of an architecture. This is contrasted with reconstitution and defensive operations, which are external to the architecture, although architectural decisions would affect the ability to reconstitute that architecture or employ defensive operations to defend it. Resilient capabilities are achievable through one or a combination of the following methodologies: disaggregation, distribution, diversification, protection, and proliferation (pp. I-8–I-9).
UFC 1-200-02	**Resiliency**—The ability to prepare for and recover from disruptions that affect mission assurance on military installations (p. 49).
	Sustainable site—Based on the selection process, a site is considered sustainable when it uses less energy, water, and natural resources; generates less waste; and minimizes the impact on land compared with conventional design, construction, and maintenance techniques (p. 52).
	Energy resiliency—The ability to prepare for and recover from energy disruptions that affect mission assurance on military installations. (DoDI 4170.11) (p. 49)

Document	Definition
	Climate change—Variations in average weather conditions that persist over multiple decades or longer, which encompass increases and decreases in temperature, shifts in precipitation, and changing risk of certain types of severe weather events. (DoDD 4715.21) (p. 48)
UFC 2-100-01	**Sustainability planning**—Meets the needs of the present without compromising the ability of future generations to meet their needs. The interrelationship between environments, resources consumed, waste products, and use of facilities and land must be designed and developed to preclude permanent damage to the future environment. In the context of a military installation, sustainability planning includes preserving the land and operating space for future mission requirements while meeting today's mission requirements (p. 85).
	Resilience—The ability to anticipate, prepare for, and adapt to changing conditions and withstand, respond to, and recover rapidly from disruptions (p. 84).
	Installation military resilience—The capability of a military installation to avoid, prepare for, minimize the effect of, adapt to, and recover from extreme weather events or from anticipated or unanticipated changes in environmental conditions, that do, or have the potential to, adversely affect the military installation or essential transportation, logistical, or other necessary resources outside the military installation that are necessary to maintain, improve, or rapidly reestablish installation mission assurance and mission-essential functions (p. 83).
	Flood hazard area—A geographic area that has been or could be inundated with water. Water inundation can be caused by multiple sources, independently or in combination, such as precipitation, snowmelt, or riverine, coastal, or tidal flooding. Common types of flood hazard areas are floodplain designations, such as the 1 percent annual chance event (ACE) or 100-year floodplain and the 0.2 percent ACE or 500-year floodplain. Flood hazard areas can also represent past flooding events (e.g., storm of significant impact) or future inundation areas reflective of sea level change scenarios (p. 82).
UFC 3-201-02	**Resiliency**—The capacity to anticipate, prepare for, respond to, recover from, and adapt to hazards and the risks they pose, including severe weather events and the effects of climate change (p. 61).

SOURCE: Features information from DAF documents.

Review of Facilities Standards

Table A.4 presents the results of a review of Air Force facilities engineering standards obtained from UFC and AFI documents relevant to wildfire and flood risk at installations.

Table A.4. Facilities Standards Documents Reviewed

Document	Publication Years of Reviewed Editions
AFI 32-1020, *Planning and Programming Built Infrastructure Projects*, Department of the Air Force, December 2019	2019–2022
AFI 32-1023, *Designing and Constructing Military Construction Projects*, Department of the Air Force, December 20, 2020	2020
AFI 90-2001, *Mission Sustainment*	2019
International Building Code (IBC)	2000–2015
International Existing Building Code (IEBC)	2015–2021
International Wildland-Urban Interface Code (IWUIC)	2015–2021
Military Handbook 1190, *Facilities Planning and Design Guide*, September 1, 1987	1987
National Fire Protection Association, *NFPA 101: Life Safety Code*, 2021.	2006–2021

Document	Publication Years of Reviewed Editions
National Fire Protection Association, *NFPA 1144: Standard for Reducing Structure Ignition Hazards from Wildland Fire*, 2018.	2002–2018
Technical Manual (TM) 5-803-01, *Installation Master Planning*, U.S. Army Corps of Engineers, June 13, 1986	1986
TM 5-803-14, *Site Planning and Design*, U.S. Army Corps of Engineers, October 14, 1994	1994
UFC 1-200-01, *DoD Building Code*	2002–2020
UFC 2-100-01, *Installation Master Planning*	2005–2020
UFC 3-201-01, *Civil Engineering*	2004–2018
UFC 3-210-06A, *Site Planning and Design*	2016
UFC 3-600-01, *Fire Protection Engineering for Facilities*, U.S. Department of Defense, updated, September 26, 2006	2003–2016

Flood

Modern engineering criteria with respect to floods originated in 1977 with EO 11988, *Floodplain Management*. EO 11988 is self-described as in furtherance of the National Environmental Policy Act (1969), National Flood Insurance Act (1968), and Flood Disaster Protection Act (1973). EO 11988 introduces many concepts that appear in relevant engineering criteria, including the following:

- Agencies must consider alternatives to proposed actions in floodplains and verify the absence of practicable alternatives prior to executing.
- Agencies must design actions within a floodplain to minimize potential harm to or within the floodplain.
- Designation of floodplain areas must be based on the best available information, such as a detailed floodplain map produced by an agency such as the Department of Housing and Urban Development (newer criteria often cite FEMA).
- Structures within floodplains must, if practicable, be elevated above the *base flood* level (the level reached by floods with a 1 percent or greater chance of occurrence within a year; also called 1 percent ACE) as opposed to filling in land.

These requirements were refined in subsequent engineering criteria. UFC 1-200-01, *DoD Building Code*, published in 2002, is the first set of relevant criteria that defers to the IBC, the first edition of which was published in 2000. Updates to UFC 1-200-01 cite updated editions of IBC. The IBC reiterates the above requirements with at least two key adjustments. IBC 2000 may have been the first criteria to apply the concept of a *design flood*—that is, the probabilistic flood that serves as the basis for engineering design. This definition of a design flood persists to the present. In the original IBC, *design flood* is defined as the greater of (1) the area of the flood of 1 percent ACE or (2) the area legally designated as a flood hazard area. In all editions of IBC, that design in flood hazard areas must conform to American Society of Civil Engineers standards 7 and 24.

The 2020 update to UFC 2-100-01, *Installation Master Planning*, with reference to designating flood hazard areas, mentions the 0.2 percent ACE flood (500-year flood) or the historical occurrence of floods as additional (of potentially many) flood hazard designations that may replace the 1 percent ACE flood for the purpose of making construction more restrictive. The 2018 update to UFC 3-201-01, *Civil Engineering*, extends the definition of design flood to allow for the use of the 0.2 percent and 1 percent ACEs as design flood events. These are not the earliest relevant references to the 500-year flood. Perhaps the earliest is Military Handbook 1190, *Facilities Planning and Design Guide*, published in 1987, which mentions that the 0.2 percent ACE should designate a floodplain for the construction of critical facilities, such as hazardous chemical storage and remote hospitals. It is unclear at which point after 1987, if ever, that superseding standards disuse the 0.2 percent ACE standard for certain building categories.

A 2015 update to UFC 1-200-01, in reference to existing buildings, requires flood hazard vulnerability analysis of mechanical and electrical systems for renovations or alterations greater than $7.5 million for structures in 1 percent ACE floodplains. This was prior to the introduction of IEBC standards for existing structures. The 2016 update to UFC 1-200-01 replaces this language with deference to the IEBC.

The development of flood engineering criteria since 1977 reveals two key shifts that stem from the 2002 introduction of language concerning design floods. The first is a shift toward more-prescriptive engineering requirements for construction within designated floodplains. The second shift captures a broadening set of planned new construction (and later, changes to existing buildings) that could be subject to the "no practicable alternatives" standard. In other words, this second shift ensures that a broader set of proposed projects would consider relocating out of the floodplain or, if not, adhering to floodplain engineering standards. Related to this second shift, the 2020 update to UFC 2-100-01 also establishes a new requirement for the use of long-term scenario analysis to envision flood risks as a function of climate change. However, specific methods for applying long-term scenario analysis have not yet been established in relevant engineering criteria. The progression of engineering standards from 1977 to the present is illustrated in Figure A.1.

Figure A.1. Timeline of the Development of Floodplain Engineering Standards Since 1977

1977: EO 11988, Floodplain Management
• "No practicable alternative" standard applies.
• 1 percent ACE standard determines minimum elevation.
• Structures must minimize harm to and within floodplain.
• Floodplain designation is based on best available information.
2002: IBC and the Design Flood
• All new floodplain construction defers to IBC for engineering standards.
• Probabilistic "design flood" serves as basis for engineering design.
• Design flood area is larger of 1 percent ACE area or any legally established area.
2015: IEBC and Engineering Standards for Existing Structures
• Specific standards are enforced for certain changes to existing structures.
2018: Expanded Design Flood Standard
• 0.2 percent ACE area can be used to designate floodplain.
• 0.2 percent ACE can be used as design flood event.
2020: Design Flood as a Function of Climate Change
• Long-term scenario analysis must inform the choice of design flood.

SOURCE: Authors' analysis of DAF documents.

Wildfire

Prior to 2006, fire protection standards for buildings did not include requirements that are contingent on the degree of wildfire risk. Fire protection standards through the first edition of UFC 3-600-01, *Fire Protection Engineering for Facilities*, applied to all DoD facilities. New buildings were required to adhere to criteria outlined in the UFC (examples are construction materials and water availability), and there were special requirements for such facilities as medical buildings and hazardous waste storage. Existing facilities are not by default required to comply with these requirements if they meet minimal requirements of NFPA 101 Life Safety Code. An exception to this condition is made for existing buildings that undergo alteration, modernization, modification, rehabilitation, [or] renovation that amounts to at least 50 percent of the replacement value of the building, in which case, the building must comply with new requirements.

In 2006, an update to UFC 3-600-01 specified special building standards for new (and, in some cases, existing) buildings within wildland. Although the general requirements and their applicability are almost identical to the previous edition, the update requires adherence to NFPA 1144, *Standard for Reducing Structure Ignition Hazards from Wildland Fire*. NFPA 1144 provides guidelines for identifying wildland ignition risks for new and existing structures within identified "wildland-urban interface" areas and sets minimum requirements for new construction in such areas.

The last update to fire protection engineering requirements related to wildfire risk follows the 2016 EO 13728 (Wildland-Urban Interface Federal Risk Mitigation), which sets requirements and recommendations for new and existing buildings constructed on federal and leased land in urban-wildland interface areas.[168] The requirements generally apply to buildings that are greater than 5,000 gross square feet in area. Importantly, EO 13728 calls for a well-characterized governance system for urban-wildland interface designation, which includes a wildfire risk rating in such areas. Updates to UFC 3-600-01, published to comply with EO 13728, require that facilities in wildland-urban interface areas adhere to the IWUIC regardless of gross square footage or land ownership. The IWUIC defines specific, logic-based conditions to determine requirements for and their applicability to new and existing buildings.

Figure A.2 depicts the development of fire protection engineering standards since before 2006 as a linear process through which the relevant policy became more specific and prescriptive over time, without negating previous measures.

---

[168] EO 13728, "Wildland-Urban Interface Federal Risk Mitigation," Executive Office of the President, May 18, 2016.

Figure A.2. Timeline of the Accumulation of Engineering Standards Since 2006

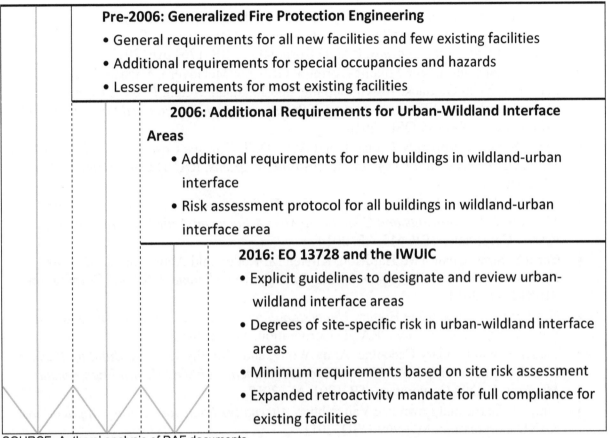

Pre-2006: Generalized Fire Protection Engineering
- General requirements for all new facilities and few existing facilities
- Additional requirements for special occupancies and hazards
- Lesser requirements for most existing facilities

2006: Additional Requirements for Urban-Wildland Interface Areas
- Additional requirements for new buildings in wildland-urban interface
- Risk assessment protocol for all buildings in wildland-urban interface area

2016: EO 13728 and the IWUIC
- Explicit guidelines to designate and review urban-wildland interface areas
- Degrees of site-specific risk in urban-wildland interface areas
- Minimum requirements based on site risk assessment
- Expanded retroactivity mandate for full compliance for existing facilities

SOURCE: Authors' analysis of DAF documents.

Organizational Comparison Documents

We reviewed the following set of RAND reports (in reverse chronological order) to compile criteria to aid in selecting the organization comparison cases presented in Chapter 4:

- Kirsten M. Keller, Maria C. Lytell, David Schulker, Kimberly Curry Hall, Louis T. Mariano, John S. Crown, Miriam Matthews, Brandon Crosby, Lisa Saum-Manning, Douglas Yeung, Leslie Adrienne Payne, Felix Knutson, and Leann Caudill, *Advancement and Retention Barriers in the U.S. Air Force Civilian White Collar Workforce: Implications for Demographic Diversity*, RAND Corporation, RR-2643-AF, 2020
- Michael Spirtas, Yool Kim, Frank Camm, Shirley M. Ross, Debra Knopman, Forrest E. Morgan, Sebastian Joon Bae, M. Scott Bond, John S. Crown, and Elaine Simmons, *A Separate Space: Creating a Military Service for Space*, RAND Corporation, RR-4263-AF, 2020
- Danielle C. Tarraf, William Shelton, Edward Parker, Brien Alkire, Diana Gehlhaus Carew, Justin Grana, Alexis Levedahl, Jasmin Léveillé, Jared Mondschein, James Ryseff, Ali Wyne, Dan Elinoff, Edward Geist, Benjamin N. Harris, Eric Hui, Cedric Kenney, Sydne Newberry, Chandler Sachs, Peter Schirmer, Danielle Schlang, Victoria Smith, Abbie Tingstad, Padmaja Vedula, and Kristin Warren, *The Department of Defense*

Posture for Artificial Intelligence: Assessment and Recommendations, RAND Corporation, RR-4229-OSD, 2019

- Mark A. Lorell, Leslie Adrienne Payne, and Karishma R. Mehta, *Program Characteristics That Contribute to Cost Growth: A Comparison of Air Force Major Defense Acquisition Programs*, RAND Corporation, RR-1761-AF, 2017

- Lisa M. Harrington, Igor Mikolic-Torreira, Geoffrey McGovern, Michael J. Mazarr, Peter Schirmer, Keith Gierlack, Joslyn Fleming, and Jonathan Welch, *Reserve Component General and Flag Officers: A Review of Requirements and Authorized Strength*, RAND Corporation, RR-1156-OSD, 2016

- Mark A. Lorell, Robert S. Leonard, and Abby Doll, *Extreme Cost Growth: Themes from Six U.S. Air Force Major Defense Acquisition Programs*, RAND Corporation, RR-630-AF, 2015

- Albert A. Robbert, Lisa M. Harrington, Tara L. Terry, and H. G. Massey, *Air Force Manpower Requirements and Component Mix: A Focus on Agile Combat Support*, RAND Corporation, RR-617-AF, 2014

- Carra S. Sims, Chaitra M. Hardison, Kirsten M. Keller, and Abby Robyn, *Air Force Personnel Research: Recommendations for Improved Alignment*, RAND Corporation, RR-814-AF, 2014

- Heather Peterson and Joe Hogler, *Understanding Country Planning: A Guide for Air Force Component Planners*, RAND Corporation, TR-1186-AF, 2012

- Thaler, David E., Gary Cecchine, Anny Wong, and Timothy Jackson, *Building Partner Health Capacity with U.S. Military Forces: Enhancing AFSOC Health Engagement Missions*, RAND Corporation, TR-1201-AF, 2012

- James T. Bartis and Lawrence Van Bibber, *Alternative Fuels for Military Applications*, RAND Corporation, MG-969-OSD, 2011

- Jennifer D. P. Moroney, Joe Hogler, Lianne Kennedy-Boudali, and Stephanie Pezard, *Integrating the Full Range of Security Cooperation Programs into Air Force Planning: An Analytic Primer*, RAND Corporation, TR-974-AF, 2011

- Melinda Moore, Michael A. Wermuth, Laura Werber, Anita Chandra, Darcy Noricks, Adam C. Resnick, Carolyn Chu, and James J. Burks, *Bridging the Gap: Developing a Tool to Support Local Civilian and Military Disaster Preparedness*, RAND Corporation, TR-764-OSD, 2010

- Michael Spirtas, Thomas Young, and S. Rebecca Zimmerman, *What It Takes: Air Force Command of Joint Operations*, RAND Corporation, MG-777-AF, 2009

- Lloyd Dixon, Chad Shirley, Laura H. Baldwin, John A. Ausink, and Nancy F. Campbell, *An Assessment of Air Force Data on Contract Expenditures*, RAND Corporation, MG-274-AF, 2005.

Appendix B. Interview Protocol

The following appendix presents background information and questions sent as read-ahead materials for interviews with AFCEC and AFIMSC personnel, and installation personnel.

AFCEC/AFIMSC Interview Background and Questions

Introduction

RAND Project AIR FORCE (PAF) is conducting research sponsored by HAF/A4C to help improve the Department of the Air Force's (DAF) understanding of installation exposure to extreme weather events and climate change-related effects, the mission risks associated with this exposure, and options for mitigating these mission risks. In particular, this project aims to provide a way for the DAF to systematically and credibly value and prioritize facility investments in improving installation and mission resilience to extreme weather and climate change. PAF will draw on prior research, analysis, tools, and data to meet this objective.

Today's discussion is intended to supplement PAF's independent review of DAF policy and guidance to understand gaps in current DAF processes and methods when it comes to identifying, evaluating, prioritizing, resourcing, or executing projects aimed at improving the resilience of DAF infrastructure to natural hazards, including the effects of climate change.

A. Background

1. What is your current role? (Rank/grade if applicable)
2. How long have you worked in this role?
3. Please describe your position in relation to the broader mission of the organization to which you belong (e.g., if AFCEC/CPPD, describe how what you personally do connects to the mission of AFCEC/CPP, AFCEC/CP, etc.)

B. Installation Planning

B.1. AFCEC, AFIMSC Roles and Responsibilities

The next several questions anchor on guidance set forth in AFI 32-1015 *Integrated Installation Planning*, which we understand serves as the primary source of guidance for installation-level planning.

AFI 32-1015 identifies several roles and responsibilities for AFCEC and AFIMSC. Among other responsibilities, our understanding is that AFIMSC is responsible for programming, budgeting, and funding of Installation and Mission Support requirements and that AFCEC executes Integrated Installation Planning Programs.

AFIMSC: 2.16.1. *"programming, budgeting, and funding the execution of Installation and Mission Support requirements, to include Program Objective Memorandum inputs for, validation of requirements, and advocacy to ensure continued installation operational capacity and capability for the enterprise.*"

AFCEC: 2.17.1.3. "*Execute Integrated Installation Planning programs (with the exception of Air Force Industrial Preparedness facilities).*"

1. Can you briefly explain what these stated responsibilities mean in practice for your respective organization? E.g., what exactly does it mean for AFCEC to "execute" programs?
2. Do AFCEC and/or AFIMSC play a role in the development of any of the installation-level plans outlined in AFI 32-1015?
3. If yes, what sort of role, and with whom do you coordinate at the installation (e.g., base civil engineers, the facilities board, planners, etc.)?
4. If no, what role does AFCEC/AFIMSC play once installations complete their plans? E.g., does AFCEC/AFIMSC review or catalog plans, or use them to support some other process or decision?
5. Beyond AFCEC/AFIMSC, what do other entities within DAF (e.g., SAF/IE, HAF/A4C) do with completed plans?
6. E.g., do installation plans directly or indirectly inform the development of the IPL or other project prioritization efforts?
7. Do you provide any other support to installations beyond those we have discussed already (i.e., those in AFI 32-1015) for installation-level planning or requirements-setting efforts? If so, can you highlight any "resilience"-focused activities which you support?

B.2. Current Planning Gaps and Needs

1. What do you see as the current gaps, whether related to data, access to information, coordination with other entities, etc., that inhibit installation-level planning or integration of plans related to infrastructure and mission resilience to natural hazards and the effects of climate change?

C. Accounting for Resilience in Project Prioritization Models and Processes

C.1. Status Quo

We would now like to discuss how resilience is or is not accounted for in project scoring models and processes. Infrastructure project prioritization processes/programs we consider relevant to our project are AFCAMP (for centralized FSRM projects), MILCON/UMMC working group (for MILCON projects), and possibly ERCIP. We will focus today's discussion on the process(es) with which you are most familiar.

C.1.1. AFCAMP

1. Are you familiar with recent updates to the AFCAMP process related to non-condition based PoF (probability of failure)? If not, can you point us to a POC who can?

2. Do you view non-condition based (NCB) probability of failure (PoF)—assigned in particular to Specific Enterprise Execution Direction (SEED)[169] projects or projects that serve Enterprise Objectives (Eos)[170]—as a method to explicitly accommodate projects' resilience aspects in the scoring model?

3. If so, please share your view of how the NCB PoF helps in accounting for the resilience value of projects.

4. Are there other elements of the AFCAMP process that accommodate explicit consideration of projects' resilience attributes, particularly related to natural hazards or climate change?

C.1.2. MILCON/UMMC

1. Is there an analog to AFCAMP NCB PoF for MILCON/UMMC projects?

2. Are there other elements of the MILCON/UMMC project prioritization process that accommodate explicit consideration of projects' resilience attributes, particularly related to natural hazards or climate change?

C.2. Current Project Prioritization Gaps and Needs

1. What additional data, information, or methods are needed to properly account for the resilience aspects of projects in current and/or future scoring models?

2. Are there organizational structures and processes in place to facilitate consideration of long-term climate risks as well as short-term natural hazards in resilience planning?

C.3. Anticipated Changes?

1. Are there any plans for changes to project prioritization processes or methods (e.g., AFCAMP or MILCON/UMMC business rules, TMDI assignment/adjudication) of which we should be aware?

2. Has there been any discussion of creating a new funding "bucket" associated with climate resilience projects, or will they compete in the same processes, e.g., AFCAMP, MILCON/UMMC working group, etc.?

3. If changes are in discussion or underway, can you share any documents (policies, guidance, etc.) related to these initiatives?

4. Is there or are there plans to use a separate prioritization process for projects tied to recovery from storms or other natural hazards? E.g., are project requests/ processes tracked in *Storm Damage Tracker*? If you cannot speak to this, can you refer us to a POC?

D. Wrap-up

1. Is there anyone else you think we should speak to about the items we discussed today?

---

[169] "are based on AF strategic direction" and "base-specific identification of requirements" through an AFIMSC governance process.

[170] "are similarly aligned with AF strategic direction but this direction does not single out a base, but are gleaned from the AF strategic master plan, other AF strategic direction, and usually one or more of AF's flight plans." Example objectives include "Mission Resiliency in Contested Environment" and "Mitigate Risk to CE Mission Essential Functions."

2. Is there anything else I didn't ask about that you think would be helpful for us to know about related to our discussion today?

E. Document Request

- Plans
- Policy documents
- Data
- Process map

F. Acronyms

AFCAMP	Air Force Comprehensive Asset Management Plan
AFCEC	Air Force Civil Engineer Center
AFI	Air Force Instruction
AFIMSC	Air Force Installation and Mission Support Center
ERCIP	Energy Resilience and Conservation Investment Program
FSRM	Facilities Sustainment, Restoration and Modernization
HAF	Headquarters Air Force
MILCON	Military Construction
TMDI	Tactical Mission dependency index
NCB	Non-condition based
PoF	Probability of failure
SAF/IE	Secretary of the Air Force, Energy, Installations and Environment
UMMC	Unspecified Minor Military Construction

Installation Interview Background and Questions

Introduction

RAND Project AIR FORCE (PAF) is conducting research sponsored by HAF/A4C to help improve the Department of the Air Force's (DAF) understanding of installation exposure to extreme weather events and climate change-related effects, the mission risks associated with this exposure, and options for mitigating these mission risks. In particular, this project aims to provide a way for the DAF to systematically and credibly value and prioritize facility investments in improving installation and mission resilience to extreme weather and climate change. PAF will draw on prior research, analysis, tools, and data to meet this objective.

Today's discussion is intended to supplement PAF's independent review of DAF policy and guidance to understand gaps in current DAF processes and methods when it comes to identifying, evaluating, prioritizing, resourcing, or executing projects aimed at improving the resilience of DAF infrastructure to natural hazards, including the effects of climate change.

A. Background

1. What is your current role? (Rank/grade if applicable)

2. How long have you worked in this role?
3. Please describe your position in relation to the broader mission of the organization to which you belong.

B. Roles and Responsibilities Related to Planning and Project Prioritization

The next several questions anchor on guidance set forth in AFI 32-1015 *Integrated Installation Planning*, which we understand serves as the primary source of guidance for installation-level planning.

AFI 32-1015 identifies several roles and responsibilities of Installation Commanders and Base Civil Engineers. Among other responsibilities, our understanding is that the Installation Commanders are required to:

2.19.10.3 . . . "Assess and manage risks associated with the effects of severe weather and a changing climate on built and natural infrastructure, in accordance with DoDD 4715.21, Climate Change Adaptation and Resilience . . ."

Likewise, among other responsibilities, Base Civil Engineers are required to:

2.32.5. Execute installation development planning . . .

2.32.5.1. Prepare, maintain and implement the Installation Development Plan.

2.32.5.2. Collect, interpret, integrate and present the vision of the Installation Commander and other senior installation leadership for mission requirements and installation development.

1. Can you briefly explain what these stated responsibilities mean in practice at your installation?

2. Do you play a role in identifying and/or prioritizing infrastructure projects at the installation-level, for inclusion in the AFCAMP or other centralized or decentralized funding process? If yes, what data/information do you use to determine whether a project should be prioritized?

C. Understanding Climate-related Risks to Installations and Missions

1. What types of data and information support your current understanding of installation exposure to severe weather events and climate change?

2. Are assets on the installation built to withstand weather- and climate-related hazards? If so, what are these standards, and to which hazards do they apply?

3. Do you think about preparing for acute climate events (i.e., a hurricane or wildfire) differently from more gradual climate impacts (i.e., sea level rise or increasing temperatures)? If so, how? If not, how might you do so?

4. Have you experienced extreme weather events, such as floods or high winds, on the installation? Based on that (or other) experience, what did you see as key impacts, or lessons learned, for mission risk mitigation?

5. What critical risks to mission operations might climate change pose?

D. Current and Planned Avenues for Integrating Climate Risk into Infrastructure Investment Decisionmaking

1. Do you participate in any working groups related to addressing resilience to extreme weather events at the installation or across installations?

2. What is your current level of community engagement or partnership in dealing with extreme weather events or preparing for climate change?
3. How is "climate resilience" or "climate resilience related-project" defined, if at all, in your planning and project execution? Do you use a definition from a specific source document?
4. Are you familiar with the Installation Climate Resilience Plans (ICRP)? If so,
5. What types of data or analysis do you intend to use to complete your ICRP?
6. How do you anticipate choosing which projects to highlight in the ICRP? Will they include already vetted projects, projects that are still in development, brand new projects, or a mix?
7. Do you view the ICRPs as a way to elevate projects whose primary value is enhancing resilience, or as a way to highlight the "resilience value" of all projects built to a given standard? Or both?
8. Based on your installation's needs (either current or projected), do you have preferences or recommendations for specific strategies to obtain resources to help achieve your resilience goals?

E. Current Gaps and Needs
1. What additional information, training, staffing, or communication do you think is needed to enhance planning and resourcing efforts related to climate resilience?

2. What would be the most useful piece of guidance from headquarters to help in your approach to improving installation resilience to climate change?

[Open discussion of any gaps and needs identified by installation personnel]

D. Wrap-up
1. Is there anyone else you think we should speak to about the items we discussed today?

2. Is there anything else I didn't ask about that you think would be helpful for us to know about related to our discussion today?

E. Document Request

- Plans
- Policy documents
- Data

Appendix C. Resilience Framework Supporting Information

This appendix provides supporting information related to the resilience project prioritization framework presented in Chapter 3.

Hazard Exposure Methodology

The DoD released DCAT in 2021 alongside an effort to complete climate exposure assessments for major CONUS installations by mid-2022 and major OCONUS installations by mid-2023.[171] The U.S. Army Corps of Engineers produced two sets of mapped riverine and coastal flood indicators using models, such as the U.S. Army Corps of Engineers River Analysis System, that intersect with an installation's topography. Independent peer review indicates that the methodology and resultant hazard exposure threshold are akin to that of FEMA's National Flood Insurance Program's Flood Insurance Rate Maps—the 1 percent AEP event as characterized by current precipitation, stream flow, and storm surge conditions.[172] Using the polygonal outlines of the 1 percent AEP-equivalent riverine floodplain provided by DISDI, we assumed that if a building was in or adjacent to a hazard area, the building is exposed to that particular hazard. However, actual exposure may be conditioned on site-specific elevation information and building construction, available via either higher resolution and classification datasets or survey.[173] The full list of installations where we intersected DCAT riverine flood data with GeoBase building footprints to assess asset-level flood exposure is shown in Figure C.1.

---

[171] DoD, "DOD Announces Installation Climate Exposure Assessments Plan Through the Defense Climate Assessment Tool," news release, April 22, 2021.

[172] Jennifer L. Bewley, Jacob B. Bartel, Shelley M. Cazares, and Sara C. Runkel, *Final Assessment of the Extreme Weather and Climate Change Vulnerability and Risk Assessment Tool*, Institute for Defense Analyses, IDA D-21598, March 2021.

[173] For instance, floodplain maps rendered via a 10-meter digital elevation model dimension are unique to DoD installations and are not available to the general public, so we do not include them in this report.

Figure C.1. Installations with DCAT Riverine Flood Data and GeoBase Building Footprints

Altus AFB	Hurlburt Field	Osan AB
Arnold AFB	Incirlik AB	Patrick AFB
Aviano AB	JB Andrews	Peterson AFB
Barksdale AFB	JB Charleston	RAF Fairford
Beale AFB	JB Elmendorf Richardson	RAF Lakenheath
Cannon AFB	JB Langley Eustis	RAF Mildenhall
Cape Cod AFS	JB McGuire Dix Lakehurst	Ramstein AB
Cheyenne Mountain SFS	JB San Antonio Fort Sam Houston	Robins AFB
Clear AFS	JB San Antonio Lackland AFB	Schriever AFB
Columbus AFB	JB San Antonio Randolph AFB	Scott AFB
Creech AFB	Keesler AFB	Seymour Johnson AFB
Davis Monthan AFB	Kirtland AFB	Shaw AFB
Dover AFB	Lajes Field	Sheppard AFB
Dyess AFB	Laughlin AFB	Spangdahlem AB
Eareckson AS	Little Rock AFB	Thule AB
Edwards AFB	Luke AFB	Tinker AFB
Eglin AFB	MacDill AFB	Travis AFB
Eielson AFB	Malmstrom AFB	Tyndall AFB
Ellsworth AFB	Maxwell AFB	US Air Force Academy
Francis E Warren AFB	McConnell AFB	Vance AFB
Goodfellow AFB	Minot AFB	Vandenberg AFB
Grand Forks AFB	Moody AFB	Whiteman AFB
Hanscom AFB	Moron AB	Wright Patterson AFB
Hill AFB	Mountain Home AFB	Yokota AB
Holloman AFB	Nellis AFB	

NOTE: Some installations, such as Offutt AFB, were not included because of data unavailability in the DCAT release as of April 2022. SFS = Space Force Station; JB = Joint Base; RAF = Royal Air Force.

To generate wildfire exposure maps, we used the publicly available FlamMap model developed by the U.S. Forest Service Missoula Fire Sciences Laboratory's Rocky Mountain Research Station[174] in combination with publicly available geospatial data on geographic traits and flammable fuel cover from the U.S. Departments of Agriculture and Interior. FlamMap, a versatile tool designed for a variety of fire and land management objectives, contains a "minimum travel time" model set that can be used to obtain conditional burn probabilities with weather and fuel moisture conditions held constant. The tool does so by simulating random fire ignitions and evaluating fuel treatments and interventions in a way that focuses on those treatments' or interventions' effectiveness absent the uncertainties of ignition sources.[175] The minimum travel time model also incorporates fire propagation via *spot fires*, or embers thrown from an active fire to ignite vegetation downwind, and *crown fire*, or fire in the canopy of trees or shrubs that advances independently of the accompanying ground fire, using either the Finney or Scott and Reinhardt models (with the latter chosen for the case studies described below).[176]

---

[174] Mark A. Finney, Stuart Brittan, Rob C. Seli, Chuck W. McHugh, and Rick Stratton, FlamMap: Fire Mapping and Analysis System, computer application, version 6.0, 2019.

[175] Seli, Brittan, and McHugh, 2019.

[176] Seli, Brittan, and McHugh, 2019.

In our analysis, we used publicly available geospatial data available from the LANDFIRE project—a shared program between the U.S. Department of Agriculture and the U.S. Department of Interior that provides wildland fire–focused geospatial data for the United States and its insular areas.[177] From this program, we used eight layers—those showing slope aspect, elevation, slope percentage, canopy bulk density, canopy base height, canopy cover, canopy height, and fuel data based on the Scott and Bergan Fire Behavior Fuel Model—to build a composite landscape file necessary to run the minimum travel time model in FlamMap.[178]

We used meteorologically determined typical red-flag warning conditions for an installation, which were held constant through each run of the model. These red-flag conditions consist of a variety of weather factors, with wind the most pertinent for FlamMap. For example, red-flag conditions at Mountain Home AFB would consist of 25 mph prevailing winds when combined with dry, late-season moisture levels.[179] Other installations may have different wind speeds (e.g., 15 mph) with different seasonality attributes, which were found using information from corresponding states or Geographic Area Coordination Centers. Additionally, we used very dry fuel moistures in each model run.[180] Finally, we used FlamMap to generate randomized ignition sources ($n = 5,000$ per 10 km model radius) to produce a burn probability map. We then defined assets as at risk of exposure to wildfire if they were within 500 feet of an area with a greater than 0.001 probability of flame impingement as determined by the burn probability map. As FlamMap is a tool with input data likely to be familiar to the AFCEC Wildland Fire Branch, in our immediate analysis, we consider the production of these maps to be within the capabilities of the DAF.

Table C.1 lists the top 10 installations considered for demonstration as flood exposure case studies in our analysis, as described in Chapter 3.

---

[177] Landfire, "About LANDFIRE," webpage, undated-a.

[178] Landfire, "LANDFIRE 2020 Mosaic Data Products," webpage, undated-b.

[179] Great Basin Coordination Center and the National Weather Service, *Interagency Annual Operating Plan for Fire Weather and Predictive Services for the Great Basin Geographic Area*, 2021.

[180] Joe H. Scott and Robert E. Burgan, *Standard Fire Behavior Fuel Models: A Comprehensive Set for Use with Rothermel's Surface Fire Spread Model*, U.S. Department of Agriculture, Forest Service, RMRS-GTR-153, 2005.

Table C.1. Installation Case Studies Considered for Flood Exposure Analysis

Installation	Percentage of Assets Exposed by Number	Percentage of Assets Exposed by PRV	Number of Exposed High TMDI Buildings (>=80)	PRV of Exposed High TMDI Buildings (>=80)
Installation E	79	84	35	$784.6M
Installation F	59	70	32	$605.9M
Installation C[a]	38	62	26	$1,125.0M
Installation G	37	53	117	$1,551.9M
Installation B[a]	29	55	40	$1,461.6M
Installation H	27	36	40	$439.1M
Installation I	26	48	25	$649.7M
Installation A[a]	23	32	22	$273.6M
Installation J	22	23	32	$195.3M
Installation K	22	53	32	$382.8M

SOURCE: DCAT, RPAD, GeoBase, TMDI, and RAND geospatial analysis.
[a] Installation was selected for case studies in Chapter 3.

Generalized Squadron Types

TMDI data identifies a squadron tenant for every asset with a RPUID attribute in GeoBase. We generalized these squadrons as shown in Figure C.2. This required several steps, for example:

- an initial fuzzy match search identified all the maintenance squadrons (i.e., AMXS, MXS, MXG).
- screening for nonstandard, but clear formulations such as "Maintenance Operations Sq" or "Aircraft Maint Sq."
- hand-coding outliers such as assets with combined ownership or nonstandard abbreviations (i.e., AMARG) after completing all the primary squadron types (e.g., communications, contracting, engineering)
- two coders in agreement disambiguating numbered squadron, wing, group, and Air Force designations into whether these were operational (flying) units or more of a headquarters-like or office function (C2, Administration, and Management).
- merging owners outside the immediate purview of the DAF (e.g., other DoD assets and services, other government entity).

We collapsed operational squadrons or specialized functions, such as different types of training and range facilities to prevent installation identification at an unclassified level.

Figure C.2. Generalized Squadron Types

C2, Administration, and Management	Operations (Mobility)
Communications Support	Operations (Special Ops)
Contracting Support	Operations Support
Engineering Support	Other DoD Assets and Services
Force Support	Other Government Entity
Intelligence and Reconnaissance	Rescue and Response
Logistics and Readiness	Research and Testing
Maintenance	Reserves and Guard
Medical Services	Security Forces
Munitions	Space Force
Operations	Tenant
Operations (Bomber)	Training and Range
Operations (Fighter)	Weather
Operations (Missile)	

Facilities Standards in Installation Case Studies

In Chapter 3, we assessed exposure of assets identified as falling within three different eras of flood and wildfire construction standards. Here we show aggregate numbers of exposed assets belonging to each of these eras at three case study installations.

Figure C.3 shows the range of asset-level flood exposure for three case study installations. The number and PRV of all buildings are totaled in bins for each of the three eras of flood engineering standards. The totals in dark blue were geospatially evaluated as having greater flood exposure per the DCAT 1 percent AEP standard. At least three observations are noteworthy. First, assets on Installations A and C face similar levels of vulnerability in terms of number of buildings built across these three periods, but the fraction of PRV attributed to vulnerable assets was proportionately greater prior to 2002. For Installation C, we can speculate that high-PRV assets were less likely to be constructed at all within a floodplain following 2002, but siting practices based on value were largely unaffected between the passage of EO 11988 in 1977 until 2002. Second, we see that a large proportion of assets in Installation B were built prior to the passage of EO 11988, and this proportion is even greater when measuring PRV. We can therefore assume that the overall risk to Installation B in the event of a severe flood is severe, as roughly one-half of the installation's value is at risk and most of the value is concentrated in assets built to a lesser minimal standard. Finally, although it appears that it is not unusual for higher-PRV assets to be disproportionately vulnerable to exposure in our demonstrative sample, this is the case to a surprising extent for construction of high-PRV assets in Installation B since 2002. This finding may suggest, if sites were understood to be exposed during their construction, that no practicable alternative to outside the floodplain exists for the construction during planning and that guidance would have recommended the assets be built to a higher engineering standard.

Figure C.3. Asset-Level Flood Exposure at Three Installations by Era of Construction

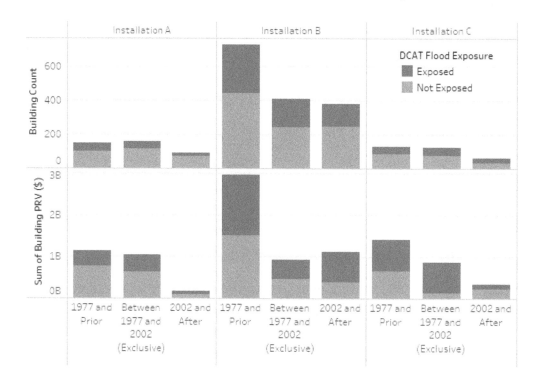

Similarly, we visualized the asset-level wildfire exposure of three case study installations (this time Installations A, B, and D) in Figure C.4. Those asset numbers and total PRV in red were evaluated as having exposure as a function of the probability of flame impingement in the event of ignition near the installation. One noteworthy observation is that the installation's PRV (as compared with asset number) is disproportionately exposed for assets constructed prior to 2006 in Installation D. In other words, in the event of nearby ignition, the smaller number of buildings that are at risk of flame impingement constitute a disproportionately high amount of PRV.

Figure C.4. Asset-Level Wildfire Exposure at Three Installations by Era of Construction

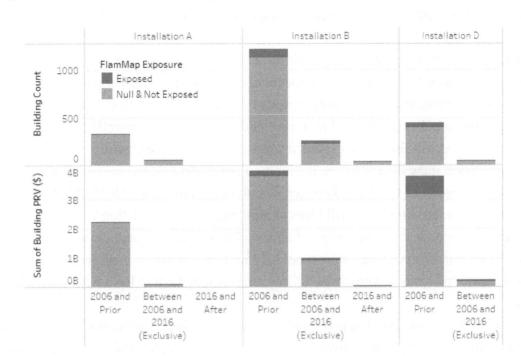

SOURCE: RPAD, GeoBase, FlamMap, LANDFIRE, and RAND geospatial analysis.
NOTE: Installation A had few buildings constructed after 2016 according to GeoBase, and Installation D had none.

Installation Hazard Risk Seasonality

To support the identification of unique unit types whose functions may not be easily replicated at other installations, a seasonality value could be incorporated into the framework as an indicator of the likelihood that different installations would be exposed to the same type of hazard at approximately the same time of year.

The season in which installations are likely to experience flooding was assumed to coincide with the season of peak streamflow.[181] Peak streamflow data from 415 stream gauge stations in the coterminous United States was downloaded from the USGS National Water Information System for a multidecadal reference period (1966–2015) during four, three-month seasonal periods: January, February, and March (JFM); April, May, and June (AMJ); July, August, and September (JAS); and October, November, and December (OND).[182] The mean peak streamflow was calculated for each gauge station in each three-month season. The season in which mean peak streamflow was highest at each station was assumed to be the season with the greatest

---

[181] J. E. Dickinson, T. M. Harden, and G. J. McCabe, "Seasonality of Climatic Drivers of Flood Air Variability in the Coterminous United States," *Scientific Reports*, Vol. 9, No. 1, 2019a.

[182] J. E. Dickinson, T. M. Harden, and G. J. McCabe, *Spatial and Temporal Variability of Peaks and Seasonal Maximum Flows in the Coterminous U.S. from Cluster Analysis of Standardized Streamflow Obtained from the USGS National Water Information System*, U.S. Geological Survey, 2019b.

likelihood of flood risk near that station. Each DAF installation was assigned the three-letter peak streamflow season value of the nearest gauge station. Installations OCONUS were omitted because of the lack of streamflow data.

We determined wildfire seasonality following a method for continuity of operations planning outlined in previous RAND work.[183] The location, date, and size of historical wildfire occurrences for a multidecadal reference period (1984–2021) were downloaded from the Monitoring Trends in Burn Severity Fire Occurrence Database.[184] Controlled burns and other fires not considered wildfires were excluded from the analysis. We classified wildfires as being near an installation if the distance from the ignition point of the fire to the location was less than or equal to one-quarter of the fire's diameter. The three-month season (JFM, AMJ, JAS, or OND) with the greatest number of wildfires in proximity to an installation was assumed to be the peak wildfire season for that installation. If an installation had an equal number of wildfire occurrences in more than one season, we assumed both seasons to be peak wildfire seasons. Installations with no historical nearby wildfires were assumed not to have a peak season for wildfires.

Table C.2 shows peak wildfire and flood seasons for CONUS installations with historical nearby wildfires. Table C.3 shows peak flood seasons for CONUS installations with no historical nearby wildfires.

---

[183] Narayanan et al., 2021.

[184] USGS and U.S. Forest Service, "Fire Occurrence Dataset, 1984-2021, Monitoring Trends in Burn Severity (MTBS) Program," 2021.

Table C.2. CONUS Installation Wildfire and Flood Peak Season

INSTALLATION NAME	WILDFIRE PEAK SEASON(S)	FLOOD PEAK SEASON
BEALE AFB	AMJ JAS	JFM
CANNON AFB	AMJ JFM	JAS
CRATER LAKE KLAMATH RGNL	JAS	JFM
ELLSWORTH AFB	JAS	AMJ
FAIRCHILD AFB	JAS	JFM
HOMESTEAD ARB	AMJ	JAS
HURLBURT FLD	JFM	JFM
JACKSONVILLE INTL	JAS	JAS
JOINT BASE MCGUIRE DIX LAKEHURST	AMJ	AMJ
LINCOLN MUNICIPAL AIRPORT	JAS	AMJ
LITTLE ROCK AFB	OND	JFM
MARCH ARB	AMJ	JFM
MCLAUGHLIN ANGB	OND	JFM
MINNEAPOLIS ST. PAUL INTL	AMJ	AMJ
MOODY AFB	OND	JAS
MOUNTAIN HOME AFB	JAS	AMJ
NAVAL BASE VENTURA COUNTY	AMJ OND	JFM
PATRICK AFB	AMJ	JAS
RENO TAHOE INTL	JAS	AMJ
SAVANNAH HILTON HEAD INTL	JFM	JAS
TINKER AFB	AMJ JFM	AMJ
TRAVIS AFB	JAS	JFM
TYNDALL AFB	JAS	JAS
USAF ACADEMY AFLD	AMJ	AMJ
VANDENBERG AFB	AMJ JAS OND	JFM

SOURCE: Features data from USGS and U.S. Forest Service.
NOTE: ANGB = air national guard base; AFLD = airfield; ARB = air reserve
base; INTL = international airport; RGNL = regional airport.

Table C.3. CONUS Installation Flood Peak Season

INSTALLATION NAME	FLOOD PEAK SEASON
ABRAHAM LINCOLN CAPITAL	AMJ
ALBUQUERQUE INTL SUNPORT	AMJ
ALPENA COUNTY RGNL	AMJ
ALTUS AFB	AMJ
ARNOLD AFB	JFM
BADER FLD	JFM
BANGOR INTL	AMJ
BARKSDALE AFB	AMJ
BATTLE CREEK EXECUTIVE AT KELLOGG FLD	AMJ

111

INSTALLATION NAME	FLOOD PEAK SEASON
BUCKLEY AFB	AMJ
CAMP BULLIS ALS	AMJ
CAPE COD	JFM
CAPE COD CGAS	JFM
CARSWELL FLD	AMJ
CHARLESTON AFB INTL	JFM
CHEYENNE RGNL JERRY OLSON FLD	AMJ
COLUMBUS AFB	JFM
CREECH AFB	AMJ
DANE CO RGNL TRUAX FLD	JFM
DAVIS MONTHAN AFB	JFM
DES MOINES INTL	AMJ
DOBBINS ARB	JFM
DOVER AFB	JFM
DYESS AFB	JAS
EARECKSON AS	OND
EASTERN WV RGNL SHEPHERD FLD	JFM
EDWARDS AFB	JFM
EGLIN AFB DESTIN FORT WALTON BEACH	JFM
JOINT RESERVE BASE ELLINGTON	AMJ
FORBES FLD	AMJ
FORT SMITH RGNL	AMJ
FORT WAYNE INTL	JFM
FRANCIS E. WARREN AFB	AMJ
FRANCIS S. GABRESKI	JFM
FRESNO YOSEMITE INTL	AMJ
GENERAL DOWNING PEORIA INTL	AMJ
GENERAL MITCHELL INTL	AMJ
GRAND FORKS AFB	AMJ
GREAT FALLS INTL	AMJ
GRISSOM ARB	AMJ
HANSCOM AFB	JFM
HARRISBURG INTL	JFM
HECTOR INTL	AMJ
HILL AFB	AMJ
HOLLOMAN AFB	AMJ
JACKSON MEDGAR WILEY EVERS INTL	JFM
JOE FOSS FLD	AMJ
JOINT BASE ANDREWS	JFM
KEESLER AFB	JFM
KELLY FLD	JAS
KEY FLD	JFM

INSTALLATION NAME	FLOOD PEAK SEASON
LANGLEY AFB	JAS
LAUGHLIN AFB	OND
LOS ANGELES INTL	JFM
LOUISVILLE MUHAMMAD ALI INTL	JFM
LUKE AFB	JFM
MACDILL AFB	JAS
MALMSTROM AFB	AMJ
MANSFIELD LAHM RGNL	JFM
MARTIN STATE	JFM
MAXWELL AFB	JFM
MCCONNELL AFB	AMJ
MCENTIRE JNGB	JFM
MCGHEE TYSON	JFM
MEMPHIS INTL	AMJ
MINOT AFB	AMJ
MOFFETT FEDERAL AFLD	JFM
MUIR AAF	JFM
NASHVILLE INTL	JFM
NELLIS AFB	AMJ
NEW CASTLE	JFM
NIAGARA FALLS INTL	JFM
OFFUTT AFB	AMJ
PETERSON FLD	JFM
PHOENIX SKY HARBOR INTL	JFM
PITTSBURGH INTL	JFM
PORTLAND INTL	JFM
PORTSMOUTH INTL AT PEASE	AMJ
QUONSET STATE	JFM
RANDOLPH AFB	AMJ
RICKENBACKER INTL	JFM
ROBINS AFB	JFM
ROSECRANS MEM	AMJ
SALT LAKE CITY INTL	AMJ
SCOTT AFB MIDAMERICA	AMJ
SELFRIDGE ANGB	JFM
SEYMOUR JOHNSON AFB	JFM
SHAW AFB	JFM
SHEPPARD AFB WICHITA FALLS MUNICIPAL	AMJ
SIOUX GATEWAY BRIG GEN BUD DAY FLD	AMJ
ST. LOUIS LAMBERT INTL	AMJ
STANLY CO	JFM
STRATTON ANGB	JFM
SYRACUSE HANCOCK INTL	AMJ

INSTALLATION NAME	FLOOD PEAK SEASON
TERRE HAUTE RGNL	AMJ
TUCSON INTL	JFM
TULSA INTL	AMJ
VANCE AFB	AMJ
VOLK FLD	AMJ
WESTOVER ARB METROPOLITAN	JFM
WHITEMAN AFB	AMJ
WRIGHT PATTERSON AFB	AMJ

SOURCE: RAND analysis of USGS data.
NOTE: CGAS = coast guard air station; AAF = army airfield.

Additional Baseline Hazard Exposure Results

For ease of interpretation in Chapter 3, we limited the case study examples to Installation A and a comparison installation. Here, we provide the baseline flood exposure data for Installation B and the baseline wildfire exposure data for Installation D (see Tables C.4 and C.5, respectively).

Table C.4. Baseline Installation B Flood Exposure

Generalized Squadron Type	Number of Exposed Assets	Percentage of Assets Exposed	PRV Exposed	TMDI Number of Exposed Assets >=80	TMDI Number of Exposed Assets with > Brief Interruptability	TMDI Number of Exposed Assets with > Extremely Difficult Replicability
C2 Administration, and Management	36	32	$356.9M	20	20	25
Communications Support	9	45	$39.1M	5	5	5
Engineering Support	113	47	$161.5M	8	14	8
Force Support	52	33	$173.2M	—	1	—
Intelligence and Reconnaissance	32	26	$31.2M	5	13	7
Logistics and Readiness	29	66	$138.5M	4	6	6
Maintenance	85	52	$330.7M	12	21	21
Medical Services	6	24	$188.3M	2	4	1
Operations	24	35	$366.9M	9	10	11
Operations Support	17	21	$118.3M	12	14	12

114

Generalized Squadron Type	Number of Exposed Assets	Percentage of Assets Exposed	PRV Exposed	TMDI		
				Number of Exposed Assets >=80	Number of Exposed Assets with > Brief Interruptability	Number of Exposed Assets with > Extremely Difficult Replicability
Other DoD Assets and Services	56	38	$123.4M	16	16	21
Other Government Entity	4	80	$10.0M	1	1	1
Research and Testing	15	50	$113.2M	5	7	5
Reserves and Guard	4	25	—	—	—	—
Security Forces	56	38	$326.2M	5	7	8
Space Force	3	19	—	1	1	1
Tenant	2	50	$2.4M	1	1	1
Training and Range	55	31	$199.6M	12	16	12
Total	**598**	**37**	**$2,679.4M**	**118**	**157**	**160**

SOURCE: DCAT, RPAD, GeoBase, TMDI, and RAND geospatial analysis.

Table C.5. Installation D Baseline Wildfire Exposure Analysis

Generalized Squadron Type	Number of Exposed Assets	Percentage of Assets Exposed	PRV Exposed	TMDI		
				Number of Exposed Assets >=80	Number of Exposed Assets with > Brief Interruptability	Number of Exposed Assets with > Extremely Difficult Replicability
C2, Administration, and Management	3	20	$18.9M	—	2	—
Communications Support	5	56	$10.7M	—	—	—
Engineering Support	10	37	$12.3M	—	—	—
Force Support	2	10	$6.3M	—	—	—
Maintenance	12	41	$28.9M	1	1	2
Medical Services	7	64	$515.9M	2	2	2
Operations	8	20	$32.1M	7	7	7
Operations Support	1	8	$0.1M	1	1	1
Other	3	43	$2.6M	—	—	1

Generalized Squadron Type	Number of Exposed Assets	Percentage of Assets Exposed	PRV Exposed	TMDI		
				Number of Exposed Assets >=80	Number of Exposed Assets with > Brief Interruptability	Number of Exposed Assets with > Extremely Difficult Replicability
Rescue and Response	2	67	$60.3M	1	1	1
Training and Range	1	33	$0.4M	—	—	—
Total	54	29	$688.5M	12	14	14

SOURCE: RPAD, GeoBase, TMDI, FlamMap, LANDFIRE, and RAND geospatial analysis.

Additional Project Exposure Reduction Results

For ease of interpretation in Chapter 3, we limited the case study examples to Installation A. Here, we describe more fully the potential exposure reduction for each of the notional projects, whose benefiting areas were shown in Chapter 3 figures.

Installation B Flood Project

Within the flood project extent, which includes more than 30 buildings, 27 buildings are included in the benefiting area based on their flood exposure. The maintenance squadron type is the largest beneficiary by building number and percentage of exposed assets benefited, with about one-half of the value-at-risk ascribed to this squadron type. In addition, the metrics in Table C.6 show that other squadron types, despite having lower exposure relative to the remainder of their buildings outside the project, may have assets that are highly mission dependent and bear additional consideration.

Table C.6. Installation B Project Flood Exposure Benefit

Generalized Squadron Type	Number of Benefiting Assets	Percentage of Exposed Assets Benefited	PRV of Benefiting Assets	TMDI		
				Number of Benefiting Assets >=80	Number of Benefited Assets with > Brief Interruptability	Number of Benefited Assets with > Extremely Difficult Replicability
Maintenance	20	24	$104.0M	4	7	5
Operational Support	2	12	$29.9M	2	2	2
Operations	2	14	$31.9M	2	2	2
Research and Testing	2	13	$27.3M	2	2	2
Training and Range	1	2	$33.4M	1	1	1
Total	**27**	**5**	**$226.6M**	**11**	**14**	**12**

SOURCE: DCAT, RPAD, GeoBase, TMDI, and RAND analysis.

Installation C Flood Project

Despite the potentially substantial cost of the Installation C flood project, Table C.7 shows a similarly large potential benefiting area. Several squadron types have most or all of their exposed assets mitigated. In particular, a few high-value (determined by both PRV and mission dependence) assets associated with the Communications squadron type, as well as wing-level C2, Administration, and Management functions, benefit from the project. It is likely that this benefit would extend beyond the installation to the entire enterprise.

Table C.7. Installation C Project Flood Exposure Benefit

Generalized Squadron Type	Number of Benefiting Assets	Percentage of Exposed Assets Benefited	PRV of Benefiting Assets	TMDI		
				Number of Benefiting Assets >=80	Number of Benefited Assets with > Brief Interruptability	Number of Benefited Assets with > Extremely Difficult Replicability
C2, Administration, and Management	7	64	$494.4M	4	4	4
Communications Support	2	29	$255.7M	2	2	2
Engineering Support	17	61	$33.2M	—	—	1
Force Support	12	44	$95.5M	—	—	—
Logistics and Readiness	9	56	$29.6M	2	3	3
Maintenance	4	100	$94.1M	2	2	2
Medical Services	1	25	$17.4M	—	—	—
Operations	5	63	$73.4M	1	1	1
Operational Support	4	67	$29.6M	1	1	—
Other DoD Assets	1	100	$0.3M	—	—	—
Reserves and Guard	2	100	$23.6M	1	1	—
Security Forces	4	44	$1.3M	1	1	1
Weather	1	100	$31.6M	1	1	1
Total	**69**	**56**	**$1,179.7M**	**15**	**16**	**16**

SOURCE: DCAT, RPAD, GeoBase, TMDI, and RAND geospatial analysis.

Installation B Wildfire Project

Figure C.5 shows the wildfire exposure after implementing the proposed perimeter road and sightline clearance project. Although additional modeling would be necessary to confirm its presence, there appears to be some *shadow effect*—the downwind or uphill areas protected by blocks treated to reduce fire ignition or spread—provided outside the immediate project boundaries because of the reduction in potential ignition points or continuous flammable area.

Figure C.5. Installation B Postproject Wildfire Exposure

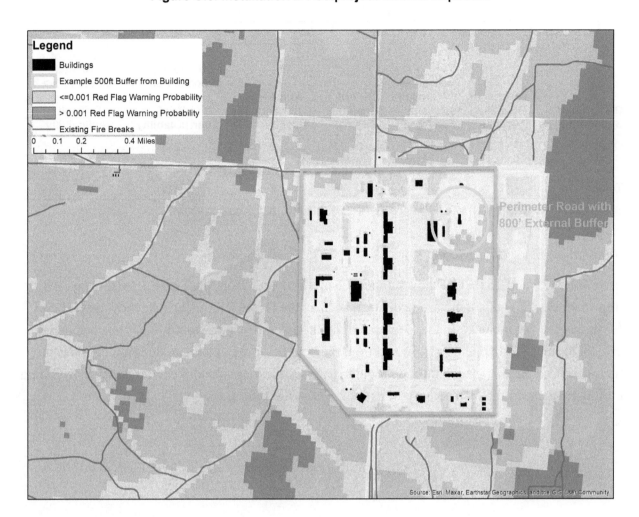

SOURCE: GeoBase, FlamMap, LANDFIRE, and RAND geospatial analysis; Maxar imagery from 2022.

Table C.8 shows that a single squadron type accrues all the benefit associated with this wildfire intervention. Further exploration, such as by applying CATCODEs, might indicate impacts to different types of functions (ranging from C2 assets to communications to logistics to maintenance, etc.) and especially those functions deemed extremely difficult to replicate relative to generalized squadron types with similar missions at different installations.

Table C.8. Installation B Project Wildfire Exposure Benefiting Area

				TMDI		
Generalized Squadron Type	Number of Benefiting Assets	Percentage of Exposed Assets Benefited	PRV of Benefiting Assets	Number of Benefiting Assets >=80	Number of Exposed Assets with > Brief Interruptability	Number of Exposed Assets with > Extremely Difficult Replicability
Operations	21	51	$137.5M	2	2	6
Total	21	51	$137.5M	2	2	6

SOURCE: RPAD, GeoBase, TMDI, FlamMap, LANDFIRE, and RAND geospatial analysis.

Installation D Wildfire Project

Figure C.6 and Table C.9 show a modest benefiting area from the Phase 1 solar array. An important caveat is that there are structures, such as the Defense Logistics Agency–owned fuel farm, that are not included in the GeoBase building inventory, that would likely be considered critical to installation operations. In addition, the benefiting area estimate does not capture the fact that this area is managed through regularly prescribed burns, and the solar panel array would eliminate the need for such activity in its footprint in the future.

Figure C.6. Installation D Phase 1 Postproject Wildfire Exposure

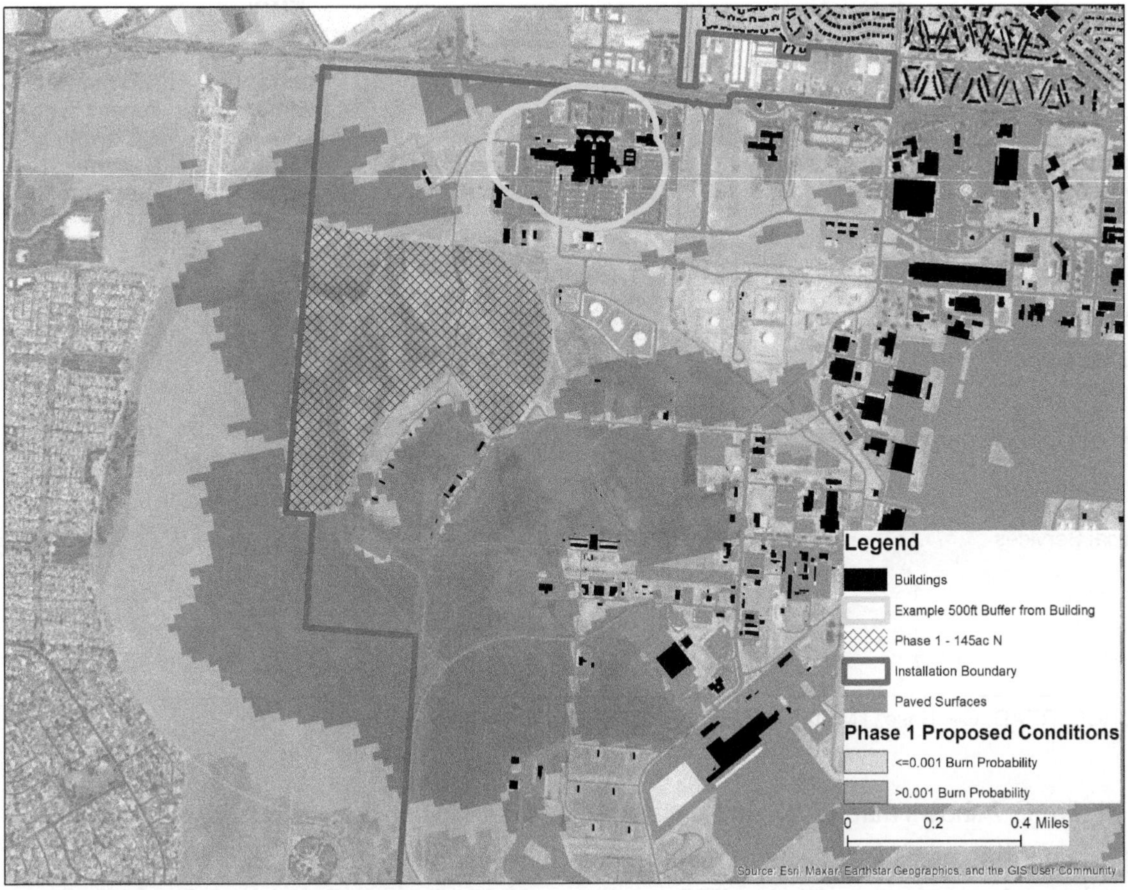

SOURCE: GeoBase, FlamMap, LANDFIRE, and RAND geospatial analysis; Maxar imagery from 2021.

Table C.9. Installation D Phase 1 Only Benefiting Area

Generalized Squadron Type	Number of Benefiting Assets	Percentage of Exposed Assets Benefited	PRV of Benefiting Assets	TMDI		
				Number of Benefiting Assets >=80	Number of Benefited Assets with > Brief Interruptability	Number of Benefited Assets with > Extremely Difficult Replicability
C2, Administration, and Management	1	33	$1.2M	—	—	—
Engineering Support	1	10	$2.3M	—	—	—
Force Support	1	50	$4.0M	—	—	1
Maintenance	1	8	$0.9M	—	—	1
Medical Services	2	29	$9.3M	1	1	1
Operations Support	1	100	$0.1M	1	1	1
Total	**7**	**13**	**$17.8M**	**2**	**2**	**4**

SOURCE: RPAD, GeoBase, TMDI, FlamMap, LANDFIRE, and RAND geospatial analysis.

Figure C.7 shows that the second phase of the solar panel array project has substantially larger benefiting areas as a result of additional reduced exposure. In Table C.10, we see that several squadron types have their wildfire exposure reduced, including the Medical Services squadron type, which has more than $500 million of benefiting assets by PRV. In addition, the operations-focused squadron types have all their exposed assets benefiting, 88 percent of which have high mission dependency.

Figure C.7. Installation D Phase 2 Postproject Wildfire Exposure

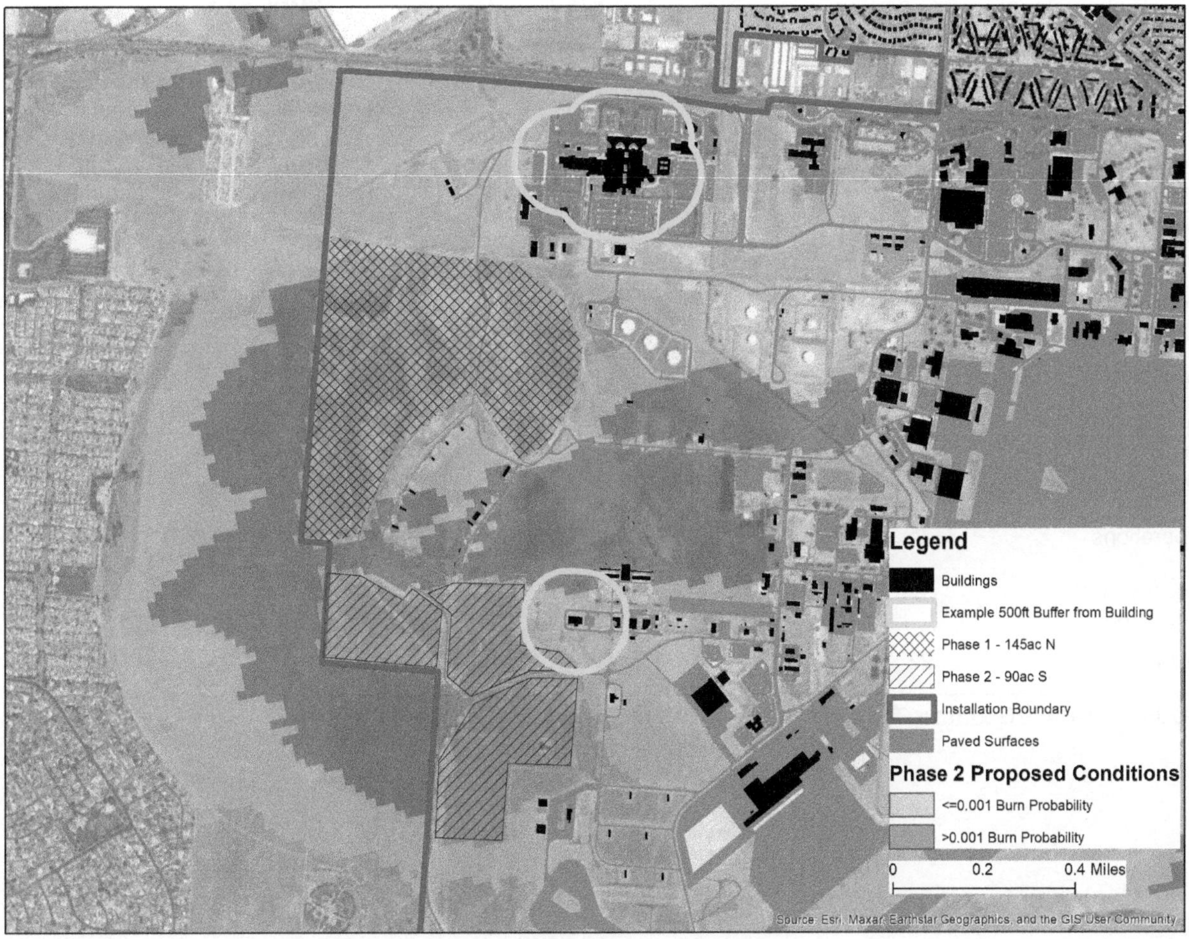

SOURCE: GeoBase, FlamMap, LANDFIRE, and RAND geospatial analysis; Maxar imagery from 2021.

Table C.10. Installation D Phase 2 Additional Benefiting Area

Generalized Squadron Type	Number of Benefiting Assets	Percentage of Exposed Assets Benefited	PRV of Benefiting Assets	Number of Benefiting Assets >=80	TMDI Number of Exposed Assets with > Brief Interruptability	Number of Exposed Assets with > Extremely Difficult Replicability
C2, Administration, and Management	1	33	$11.8M	—	—	—
Communications Support	2	40	$6.9M	—	—	—
Engineering Support	3	30	$4.7M	—	—	—
Maintenance	1	8	$0.9M	—	—	1
Medical Services	5	71	$508.4M	2	2	2
Operations	8	100	$32.1M	7	7	7
Rescue and Response	2	2	$60.3M	1	1	1
Total	**22**	**41**	**$625.1M**	**10**	**10**	**11**

SOURCE: RPAD, GeoBase, TMDI, FlamMap, LANDFIRE, and RAND geospatial analysis.

Appendix D. Factors Contributing to Climate Uncertainty

In this appendix, we provide a summary of three primary factors that contribute to the uncertainty in future climate projections: natural variability, model-based uncertainty, and future scenario–based uncertainty. We also discuss over what temporal and spatial scales these different sources of uncertainty are most influential.

Natural Variability

There is inherent uncertainty in the weather conditions that a location experiences on any given day. This variability is a natural consequence of the chaotic systems that interplay with one another in the climate system and is often referred to as natural variability. This source of uncertainty can dominate on shorter timescales (e.g., days to decades) and for specific locations (e.g., subcontinental).[185] Uncertainties associated with natural variability will remain even as climate science continues to make advances that improve model accuracy and the plausibility of climate scenarios.[186]

Model Uncertainty

To understand the potential impacts of climate change, scientists build and run GCMs. These are physics-based computer models that simulate atmospheric physics and chemistry, as well as their interaction with land and sea ice.[187] There are dozens of these models with different assumptions and representations of physical processes. The Coupled Model Intercomparison Project (CMIP) is a collaborative effort among climate scientists to standardize these GCMs and make their results publicly available. The set of models that were used in recent assessments of climate change impacts (e.g., the Fourth National Climate Assessment) came from CMIP5, the project's fifth phase.[188] A new set of models (CMIP6) was developed in 2018, and they are currently being integrated into ongoing assessments, such as the Fifth National Climate Assessment.[189]

---

[185] Clara Deser, Reto Knutti, Susan Solomon, and Adam S. Phillips, "Communication of the Role of Natural Variability in Future North American Climate," *Nature Climate Change*, Vol. 2, No. 11, 2012.

[186] Ed Hawkins and Rowan Sutton, "The Potential to Narrow Uncertainty in Regional Climate Predictions," *Bulletin of the American Meteorological Society*, Vol. 90, No. 8, 2009.

[187] USGCRP, 2018, Chapter 2, Key Message 10.

[188] USGCRP, 2018.

[189] Samantha Basile, Fred Lipschultz, Kenneth Kunkel, David R. Easterling, and Allison Crimmins, "Downscaled CMIP6 Datasets in the Fifth National Climate Assessment," *American Geophysical Union Fall Meeting*, 2022.

Despite the advances that have been made in GCMs over the past several decades, there are limitations to these models. As with any model of something as complex as an entire planet and its atmosphere, there are some physical processes that are not well captured (e.g., simulating clouds).[190] Additionally, GCMs have limited spatial resolution. To get climate model results to resolutions that are more relevant for decisionmaking, scientists create regional climate models using various downscaling methods. These models use the outputs from many GCMs as boundary conditions and provide results at higher spatial resolution (e.g., 1–2 km grids).[191] Although these RCMs provide additional resolution and, depending on the downscaling method, can be more closely linked to historical climate observations or provide some additional insight into physical processes at smaller spatial scales, they do not remove all limitations built into the GCMs that are relevant for understanding the impacts of climate at the local level.[192] A compounding issue is that global and regional-scale climate models have a tendency to smooth out precipitation events over the year, so although they may be adequately projecting annual increases in rainfall, they are not capable of resolving and projecting the occurrence of extreme precipitation events.[193]

Generally, climate models are successful at modeling changes to surface temperatures but do not do as well at simulating large-scale precipitation patterns and struggle with representing the frequency of extreme precipitation events.[194]

Future Scenarios

Running these climate models requires making assumptions about the future. To do so, the climate science community employs a scenario-based approach by developing several scenarios with assumed trajectories for such variables as the amount of GHG emissions, land use, and land cover that can then be used as inputs for the GCMs. These scenarios do not have probabilities associated with them but are instead intended to represent a variety of potential future conditions.[195]

---

[190] IPCC, *Climate Change 2013: The Physical Science Basis*, Cambridge University Press, 2013, p. 743.

[191] USGCRP, *Climate Science Special Report: Fourth National Climate Assessment, Volume I*, 2017, Chapter 4.2.1.

[192] USGCRP, 2018, Chapter 2, Key Message 10.

[193] D. A. Randall, R. A. Wood, S. Bony, R. Colman, T. Fichefet, J. Fyfe, V. Kattsov, A. Pitman, J. Shukla, J. Srinivasan, R. J. Stouffer, A. Sumi, and K. E. Taylor, "Climate Models and Their Evaluation," in S. Solomon, D. Qin, M. Manning, Z. Chen, M. Marquis, K. B. Averyt, M. Tignor, and H. L. Miller, eds., *Climate Change 2007: The Physical Science Basis*, Cambridge University Press, 2007, p. 628.

[194] IPCC, 2013, pp. 743–744.

[195] USGCRP, 2017, Chapter 4.2.1.

Commonly used scenarios are the Representative Concentration Pathways 4.5 and 8.5, which were developed to support the United Nations' IPCC Fifth Assessment Report.[196] They are a set of scenarios that describe potential pathways for amounts of GHGs and other relevant concentrations of atmospheric particles and how land use and cover may change in the future.[197]

The uncertainty that follows from using these scenarios results from our inability to predict the exact conditions of the future and to know which particular scenario is the best estimate of future conditions. Additional uncertainty is introduced for longer timescale scenarios, particularly when considering time frames beyond 2050. This is because the climate projections mostly agree until that point, but diverge afterward, making the selection and application of a scenario for 2050 and onward more significant. Therefore, the dominant sources of uncertainty in the near-term time frame come from the choice of global or regional climate models and natural variability. However, as one looks further into the future, most of the uncertainty in climate projections stems from the uncertainty associated with both the reliability and selection of the scenarios.[198]

---

[196] Intergovernmental Panel on Climate Change, *Climate Change 2014: Synthesis Report—Contribution of Working Groups I, II, and III to the Fifth Assessment Report of the Intergovernmental Panel on Climate Change*, 2014.

[197] L. Briley R. Dougherty, K. Wells, T. Hercula, M. Notaro, R. Rood, J. Andresen, F. Marsik, A. Prosperi, J. Jorns, K. Channell, S. Hutchinson, C. Kemp, and O. Gates, eds., *A Practitioner's Guide to Climate Model Scenarios*, Great Lakes Integrated Sciences and Assessments, 2021.

[198] Hawkins and Sutton 2009, p. 1096.

Abbreviations

ACE	annual chance event
AEP	annual exceedance probability
AFB	Air Force Base
AFCAMP	Air Force Comprehensive Asset Management Plan
AFCEC	Air Force Civil Engineer Center
AFDP	Air Force Doctrine Publication
AFI	Air Force Instruction
AFIMSC	Air Force Installation and Mission Support Center
AFPD	Air Force Policy Directive
AMJ	April, May, and June
AMXS	Aircraft Maintenance Squadron
API	asset priority index
AREA	Absorptive, Restorative, Equitable Access and Adaptive
BIRB	Bureau Investment Review Board
BRIC	Building Resilient Infrastructure and Communities
C2	command and control
CATCODE	Category Code
CDP	Carbon Disclosure Project
CFE	carbon-free energy
CMIP	Coupled Model Intercomparison Project
CONUS	continental United States
CPP	Comprehensive Planning Division
DAF	Department of the Air Force
DCAT	Defense Climate Assessment Tool
DISDI	Defense Installations Spatial Data Infrastructure
DoD	U.S. Department of Defense
DoDD	Department of Defense Directive
DoDI	Department of Defense Instruction
DRRS-S	Defense Readiness Reporting System-Strategic
EO	Executive Order
ERM	Enterprise Risk Management
ESG	environmental, social, and governance
FEMA	Federal Emergency Management Agency
FSRM	Facilities Sustainment, Restoration, and Modernization
FY	fiscal year

GAO	U.S. Government Accountability Office
GCM	global climate model
GHG	greenhouse gas
GSO	Google sustainability officer
HAF	Headquarters Air Force
IBC	International Building Code
ICRP	Installation Climate Resilience Plan
IDP	Installation Development Plan
IEBC	International Existing Building Code
IPCC	Intergovernmental Panel on Climate Change
IPL	integrated priority list
IWUIC	International Wildland-Urban Interface Code
JAS	July, August, and September
JFM	January, February, and March
JP	Joint Publication
MAJCOM	major command
MILCON	military construction
MIRTA	military installations, ranges, and training areas
MXG	Maintenance Group
NAVFAC	Naval Facilities Engineering Systems Command
NCB	noncondition based
NFPA	National Fire Protection Association
NOFO	Notice of Funding Opportunity
NPS	National Park Service
OCONUS	outside the continental United States
OND	October, November, and December
PAF	Project AIR FORCE
PoF	probability of failure
PRV	plant replacement value
RDVM	Resilience Dividend Valuation Model
RPAD	Real Property Asset Database
RPUID	Real Property Unique Identifier
SAF/IE	Secretary of the Air Force, Energy, Installations, and Environment
SME	subject-matter expert
SWP	Severe Weather Playbook
TM	Technical Manual
TMDI	Tactical Mission Dependency Index
UFC	Unified Facilities Criteria
UMMC	unspecified minor military construction

USGS	U.S. Geological Survey
USGCRP	U.S. Global Change Research Program

References

Adger, W. Neil, "Social and Ecological Resilience: Are They Related?" *Progress in Human Geography*, Vol. 24, No. 3, 2000.

AFDP—*See* Air Force Doctrine Publication.

AFI—*See* Air Force Instruction.

AFPD—*See* Air Force Policy Directive.

Ahmed, Rashid, Mohamed Seedat, Ashley van Niekerk, and Samed Bulbulia, "Discerning Community Resilience in Disadvantaged Communities in the Context of Violence and Injury Prevention," *South African Journal of Psychology*, Vol. 34, No. 3, 2004.

Air Force Doctrine Publication 3-59, *Weather Operations*, Curtis E. LeMay Center for Doctrine Development and Education, October 28, 2020.

Air Force Instruction 32-1015, *Integrated Installation Planning*, Department of the Air Force, July 30, 2019, corrective action, January 4, 2021.

Air Force Instruction 32-1020, *Planning and Programming Built Infrastructure Projects,* Department of the Air Force, December 2019.

Air Force Instruction 32-1023, *Designing and Constructing Military Construction Projects*, Department of the Air Force, December 20, 2020.

Air Force Instruction 32-7020, *Environmental Restoration Program,* Department of the Air Force, March 2020.

Air Force Instruction 32-7091, *Environmental Management Outside the United States*, Department of the Air Force, November 2019.

Air Force Instruction 90-802, *Risk Management*, Department of the Air Force, April 1, 2019.

Air Force Instruction 90-1701, *Installation Energy and Water Management*, Department of the Air Force, April 1, 2019.

Air Force Instruction 90-2001, *Mission Sustainment*, Department of the Air Force, July 31, 2019.

Air Force Manual 15-129, *Air and Space Weather Operations*, Department of the Air Force, July 2020.

Air Force Manual 32-7003, *Environmental Conservation*, Department of the Air Force, April 2020.

Air Force Policy Directive 32-10, *Installations and Facilities*, Department of the Air Force, July 2020.

Air Force Policy Directive 32-70, *Environmental Considerations in Air Force Programs and Activities*, Department of the Air Force, July 2018.

Air Force Policy Directive 90-17, *Energy and Water Management*, Department of the Air Force, May 2020.

Air Force Policy Directive 90-20, *Mission Sustainment*, Department of the Air Force, April 18, 2019.

Alphabet CDP Climate Change Response 2021, Climate Disclosure Project, July 2021.

AquaFence, "Flood Wall," webpage, undated. As of September 27, 2022:
https://www.aquafence.com/floodwall/

Army Directive 2020-08, *U.S. Army Installation Policy to Address Threats Caused by Changing Climate and Extreme Weather*, Secretary of Defense, September 11, 2020.

Bartis, James T., and Lawrence Van Bibber, *Alternative Fuels for Military Applications*, RAND Corporation, MG-969-OSD, 2011. As of September 27, 2022:
https://www.rand.org/pubs/monographs/MG969.html

Basile, Samantha, Fred Lipschultz, Kenneth Kunkel, David R. Easterling, and Allison Crimmins, "Downscaled CMIP6 Datasets in the Fifth National Climate Assessment," *American Geophysical Union Fall Meeting*, 2022.

Bewley, Jennifer L., Jacob B. Bartel, Shelley M. Cazares, and Sara C. Runkel, *Final Assessment of the Extreme Weather and Climate Change Vulnerability and Risk Assessment Tool*, Institute for Defense Analyses, IDA D-21598, March 2021.

Bhoite, Sachin, Kieran Birtill, Stephen Cook, Sandra Diaz, Vicky Evans, Andrea Fernandez, Laura Frost, Sam Kernaghan, Ashlee Loiacono, Braulio Eduardo Morera, Geoffrey Morgan, Elizabeth Parker, Jo da Silva, Samantha Stratton-Short, and Flora Tonking, *City Resilience Framework*, Arup International Development, updated December 2015.

Bierman, S., B. Graf, and M. Akers, "CPI-Driven FY24 AFCAMP Business Rule Changes," unclassified Department of the Air Force briefing, 2022.

Bodin, Per, and Bo L. B. Wiman, "Resilience and Other Stability Concepts in Ecology: Notes on Their Origin, Validity, and Usefulness," *ESS Bulletin*, Vol. 2, No. 2, 2004.

Bond, Craig A., Aaron Strong, Nicholas E. Burger, and Sarah Weilant, *Guide to the Resilience Dividend Valuation Model*, RAND Corporation, RR-2130-RF, 2017. As of September 27, 2022:
https://www.rand.org/pubs/research_reports/RR2130.html

Bond, Craig A., Aaron Strong, Nicholas E. Burger, Sarah Weilant, Uzaib Saya, and Anita Chandra, *Resilience Dividend Valuation Model: Framework Development and Initial Case Studies*, RAND Corporation, RR-2129-RF, 2017. As of September 27, 2022: https://www.rand.org/pubs/research_reports/RR2129.html

Briley, L., R. Dougherty, K. Wells, T. Hercula, M. Notaro, R. Rood, J. Andresen, F. Marsik, A. Prosperi, J. Jorns, K. Channell, S. Hutchinson, C. Kemp, and O. Gates, eds., *A Practitioner's Guide to Climate Model Scenarios*, Great Lakes Integrated Sciences and Assessments, 2021.

Brosam, Daniel, "Malmstrom AFB Receives New Fire Truck," *Air Force News*, July 12, 2017.

Brown, David D., and Judith Celene Kulig, "The Concepts of Resiliency: Theoretical Lessons from Community Research," *Health and Canadian Society*, Vol. 4, No. 1, 1996–1997.

Bruneau, Michel, Stephanie E. Chang, Ronald T. Eguchi, George C. Lee, Thomas D. O'Rourke, Andrei M. Reinhorn, Masanobu Shinozuka, Kathleen Tierney, William A. Wallace, and Detlof Von Winterfeldt, "A Framework to Quantitatively Assess and Enhance the Seismic Resilience of Communities," *Earthquake Spectra*, Vol. 19, No. 4, 2003.

Butler, Lisa D., Leslie A. Morland, and Gregory A. Leskin, "Psychological Resilience in the Face of Terrorism," in Bruce Bongar, Lisa M. Brown, Larry E. Beutler, James N. Breckenridge, and Philip G. Zimbardo, eds., *Psychology of Terrorism*, Oxford University Press, 2007.

Carbon Disclosure Project Worldwide, *FedEx Corporation—Climate Change 2021*, July 2021.

Carpenter, Steve, Brian Walker, J. Marty Anderies, and Nick Abel, "From Metaphor to Measurement: Resilience of What to What?" *Ecosystems*, Vol. 4, 2001.

Center for Climate and Security, *Background Paper on Top 10 Air Force Bases at Risk of Weather Impacts*, undated.

Clancy, Noreen, Melissa L. Finucane, Jordan R. Fischbach, David G. Groves, Debra Knopman, Karishma V. Patel, and Lloyd Dixon, *The Building Resilient Infrastructure and Communities Mitigation Grant Program: Incorporating Hazard Risk and Social Equity into Decisionmaking Processes*, Homeland Security Operational Analysis Center operated by the RAND Corporation, RR-A1258-1, 2022. As of September 26, 2022: https://www.rand.org/pubs/research_reports/RRA1258-1.html

Coles, Eve, and Philip Buckle, "Developing Community Resilience as a Foundation for Effective Disaster Recovery," *Australian Journal of Emergency Management*, Vol. 19, No. 4, November 2004.

Correll, Mark, "Where Mission Assurance Meets Energy Assurance," *Military Engineer*, Vol. 113, No. 72, March–April 2021.

Council on Strategic Risks and the Center for Climate and Security, *Climate Change and the National Defense Authorization Act*, June 2022.

DAF—See Department of the Air Force.

Department of the Air Force, *Installation Energy Strategic Plan*, U.S. Department of Defense, 2021.

Department of the Air Force, *Fiscal Year 2023 Budget Overview*, March 28, 2022a.

Department of the Air Force, *Department of the Air Force Climate Action Plan*, Office of the Assistant Secretary for Energy, Installations, and Environment, October 2022b.

Department of the Army, *Army Installations Strategy*, December 2020.

Department of the Army, *United States Army Climate Strategy*, February 2022.

Department of Defense Directive 3020.40, *Mission Assurance*, U.S. Department of Defense, change 1, September 11, 2018.

Department of Defense Directive 4715.21, *Climate Change Adaptation and Resilience*, U.S. Department of Defense, January 14, 2016.

Department of Defense Instruction 3200.21, *Sustaining Access to the Live Training Domain*, U.S. Department of Defense, incorporating change 1, July 2, 2020.

Department of Defense Instruction 4170.11, *Installation Energy Management*, U.S. Department of Defense, December 11, 2009.

Deser, Clara, Reto Knutti, Susan Solomon, and Adam S. Phillips, "Communication of the Role of Natural Variability in Future North American Climate," *Nature Climate Change*, Vol. 2, No. 11, 2012.

Dickinson, J. E., T. M. Harden, and G. J. McCabe, "Seasonality of Climatic Drivers of Flood Air Variability in the Coterminous United States," *Scientific Reports*, Vol. 9, No. 1, 2019a.

Dickinson, J. E., T. M. Harden, and G. J. McCabe, *Spatial and Temporal Variability of Peaks and Seasonal Maximum Flows in the Coterminous U.S. from Cluster Analysis of Standardized Streamflow Obtained from the USGS National Water Information System*, U.S. Geological Survey, 2019b.

Dixon, Lloyd, Chad Shirley, Laura H. Baldwin, John A. Ausink, and Nancy F. Campbell, *An Assessment of Air Force Data on Contract Expenditures*, RAND Corporation, MG-274-AF, 2005. As of September 27, 2022:
https://www.rand.org/pubs/monographs/MG274.html

DoDD—*See* Department of Defense Directive.

DoDI—*See* Department of Defense Instruction.

Egeland, Byron, Elizabeth Carlson, and L. Alan Sroufe, "Resilience as Process," *Development and Psychopathology*, Vol. 5, No. 4, October 1993.

EO—*See* Executive Order.

Executive Order 11988, "Floodplain Management," Executive Office of the President, May 24, 1977.

Executive Order 13728, "Wildland-Urban Interface Federal Risk Mitigation," Executive Office of the President, May 18, 2016.

Federal Emergency Management Agency, "About BRIC: Reducing Risk Through Hazard Mitigation," webpage, undated. As of September 27, 2022: https://www.fema.gov/grants/mitigation/building-resilient-infrastructure-communities/about

Federal Emergency Management Agency, "New Geospatial File Eligibility Criteria in Flood Mitigation Grant Applications," June 2020.

Federal Emergency Management Agency, *Department of Homeland Security Notice of Funding Opportunity Fiscal Year 2021 Building Resilient Infrastructure and Communities*, 2021a.

Federal Emergency Management Agency, *Department of Homeland Security Notice of Funding Opportunity Fiscal Year 2021 Flood Mitigation Assistance*, 2021b.

Federal Emergency Management Agency, "Where Equity Fits into the BRIC/FMA Program Design and Community Resilience," BRIC and FMA Program Webinar Series, August 18, 2021c.

Federal Emergency Management Agency, *BRIC Technical Criteria*, FEMA program support material, August 2021d.

Federal Emergency Management Agency, *Resources for Climate Resilience*, December 2021e.

FEMA—*See* Federal Emergency Management Agency.

Finney, Mark A., Stuart Brittan, Rob C. Seli, Chuck W. McHugh, and Rick Stratton, FlamMap: Fire Mapping and Analysis System, computer application, version 6.0, 2019.

Fischbach, Jordan R., Kyle Siler-Evans, Devin Tierney, Michael T. Wilson, Lauren M. Cook, and Linnea Warren May, *Robust Stormwater Management in the Pittsburgh Region: A Pilot Study*, RAND Corporation, RR-1673-MCF, 2017. As of September 27, 2022: https://www.rand.org/pubs/research_reports/RR1673.html

Fischbach, Jordan R., Michael T. Wilson, Craig A. Bond, Ajay K. Kochhar, David Catt, and Devin Tierney, *Managing Heavy Rainfall with Green Infrastructure: An Evaluation in Pittsburgh's Negley Run Watershed*, RAND Corporation, RR-A564-1, 2020. As of September 27, 2022: https://www.rand.org/pubs/research_reports/RRA564-1.html

Flood Control International, "Flood Barriers," webpage, undated. As of September 27, 2022: https://floodcontrolinternational.com/flood-barriers/

Francis, Royce, and Behailu Bekera, "A Metric and Frameworks for Resilience Analysis of Engineered and Infrastructure Systems," *Reliability Engineering & System Safety*, Vol. 121, January 2014.

Ganor, Michael, and Yuli Ben-Lavy, "Community Resilience: Lessons Derived from Gilo Under Fire," *Journal of Jewish Communal Service*, Winter/Spring, 2003.

Godschalk, David R., "Urban Hazard Mitigation: Creating Resilient Cities," *Natural Hazards Review*, Vol. 4, No. 3, August 2003.

Google, *24/7 Carbon-Free Energy: Methodologies and Metrics*, February 2021.

Gordon, J. E., *Structures*, Penguin Books, 1978.

Gould, Joe, "Storm-Ravaged Bases Wait on Washington for Repair Money," *Defense News*, May 10, 2019.

Great Basin Coordination Center and the National Weather Service, Interagency Annual Operating Plan for Fire Weather and Predictive Services for the *Great Basin Geographic Area*, 2021.

Harrington, Lisa M., Igor Mikolic-Torreira, Geoffrey McGovern, Michael J. Mazarr, Peter Schirmer, Keith Gierlack, Joslyn Fleming, and Jonathan Welch, *Reserve Component General and Flag Officers: A Review of Requirements and Authorized Strength*, RAND Corporation, RR-1156-OSD, 2016. As of September 27, 2022: https://www.rand.org/pubs/research_reports/RR1156.html

Hawkins, Ed, and Rowan Sutton, "The Potential to Narrow Uncertainty in Regional Climate Predictions," *Bulletin of the American Meteorological Society*, Vol. 90, No. 8, 2009.

Holling, C. S., "Resilience and Stability of Ecological Systems," *Annual Review of Ecology and Systematics*, Vol. 4, No. 1, 1973.

Hudson, Christina, and Greg Hammer, *Addressing Severe Weather and Climate Threats at Installations from a Planning Perspective*, Air Force Installation and Mission Support Center, May 2021.

Interagency Fuel Treatment Decision Support System Help Center, "Technical Documentation—Landscape Burn Probability with FlamMap," webpage, undated. As of September 27, 2022: https://iftdss.firenet.gov/firenetHelp/help/pageHelp/content/20-models/lbp/techdoclbp.htm

Intergovernmental Panel on Climate Change, *Climate Change 2013: The Physical Science Basis*, Cambridge University Press, 2013.

Intergovernmental Panel on Climate Change, *Climate Change 2014: Synthesis Report—Contribution of Working Groups I, II, and III to the Fifth Assessment Report of the Intergovernmental Panel on Climate Change*, 2014.

Intergovernmental Panel on Climate Change, "Summary for Policymakers," in V. Masson-Delmotte, P. Zhai, A. Pirani, S. L. Connors, C. Péan, S. Berger, N. Caud, Y. Chen, L. Goldfarb, M. I. Gomis, M. Huang, K. Leitzell, E. Lonnoy, J. B. R. Matthews, T. K. Maycock, T. Waterfield, O. Yelekçi, R. Yu, and B. Zhou, eds., *Climate Change 2021: The Physical Science Basis*, Cambridge University Press, 2021.

IPCC—*See* Intergovernmental Panel on Climate Change.

Joint Publication 1-02, *Department of Defense Dictionary of Military and Associated Terms*, amended November 15, 2012.

Joint Publication 3-14, *Space Operations*, change 1, April 10, 2018, Joint Chiefs of Staff, October 26, 2020.

JP—*See* Joint Publication.

Keller, Kirsten M., Maria C. Lytell, David Schulker, Kimberly Curry Hall, Louis T. Mariano, John S. Crown, Miriam Matthews, Brandon Crosby, Lisa Saum-Manning, Douglas Yeung, Leslie Adrienne Payne, Felix Knutson, and Leann Caudill, *Advancement and Retention Barriers in the U.S. Air Force Civilian White Collar Workforce: Implications for Demographic Diversity*, RAND Corporation, RR-2643-AF, 2020. As of September 26, 2022: https://www.rand.org/pubs/research_reports/RR2643.html

Kimhi, Shaul, and Michal Shamai, "Community Resilience and the Impact of Stress: Adult Response to Israel's Withdrawal from Lebanon," *Journal of Community Psychology*, Vol. 32, No. 4, July 2004.

Klein, Richard J. T., Robert J. Nicholls, and Frank Thomalla, "Resilience to Natural Hazards: How Useful Is This Concept?" *Global Environmental Change*, Part B: *Environmental Hazards*, Vol. 5, Nos. 1–2, 2003.

Kolesar, Peter, *A Model for Predicting Average Fire Company Travel Times*, RAND Corporation, R-1624-NYC, 1975. As of April 4, 2023: https://www.rand.org/pubs/reports/R1624.html

Landfire, "About LANDFIRE," webpage, undated-a. As of September 27, 2022: https://www.landfire.gov/about.php

Landfire, "LANDFIRE 2020 Mosaic Data Products," webpage, undated-b. As of September 27, 2022: https://www.landfire.gov/version_download.php

"Large-Scale Prescribed Burn Near Hurlburt Field Jan. 30," *Air Force News*, January 29, 2021.

Lempert, Robert J., Steven W. Popper, and Steven C. Bankes, *Shaping the Next One Hundred Years: New Methods for Quantitative, Long-Term Policy Analysis*, RAND Corporation, MR-1626-RPC, 2003. As of September 27, 2022:
https://www.rand.org/pubs/monograph_reports/MR1626.html

Londono, Juliana, "Two Years After a Flood, the 9th PSPTS Reopens," *Air Force News*, August 20, 2021.

Longstaff, Patricia H., *Security, Resilience, and Communication in Unpredictable Environments Such as Terrorism, Natural Disasters, and Complex Technology*, Center for Information Policy Research, Harvard University, November 2005.

Lorell, Mark A., Robert S. Leonard, and Abby Doll, *Extreme Cost Growth: Themes from Six U.S. Air Force Major Defense Acquisition Programs*, RAND Corporation, RR-630-AF, 2015. As of September 27, 2022:
https://www.rand.org/pubs/research_reports/RR630.html

Lorell, Mark A., Leslie Adrienne Payne, and Karishma R. Mehta, *Program Characteristics That Contribute to Cost Growth: A Comparison of Air Force Major Defense Acquisition Programs*, RAND Corporation, RR-1761-AF, 2017. As of September 27, 2022:
https://www.rand.org/pubs/research_reports/RR1761.html

Losey, Stephen, "After Massive Flood, Offutt Looks to Build a Better Base," *Air Force Times*, August 7, 2020.

Masten, Ann S., Karin M. Best, and Norman Garmezy, "Resilience and Development: Contributions from the Study of Children Who Overcome Adversity," *Development and Psychopathology*, Vol. 2, No. 4, October 1990.

Military Handbook 1190, *Facilities Planning and Design Guide*, Military and Government Specs and Standards, Naval Publications and Form Center, September 1, 1987.

Mills, Patrick, Muharrem Mane, Kenneth Kuhn, Anu Narayanan, James D. Powers, Peter Buryk, Jeremy M. Eckhause, John G. Drew and Kristin F. Lynch, *Articulating the Effects of Infrastructure Resourcing on Air Force Missions: Competing Approaches to Inform the Planning, Programming, Budgeting, and Execution System*, RAND Corporation, RR-1578-AF, 2017. As of April 5, 2023:
https://www.rand.org/pubs/research_reports/RR1578.html

Miro, Michelle E., Andrew Lauland, Rahim Ali, Edward W. Chan, Richard H. Donohue, Liisa Ecola, Timothy R. Gulden, Liam Regan, Karen M. Sudkamp, Tobias Sytsma, Michael T. Wilson, and Chandler Sachs, *Assessing Risk to the National Critical Functions as a Result of Climate Change*, Homeland Security Operational Analysis Center operated by the RAND Corporation, RR-A1645-7, 2022. As of September 26, 2022: https://www.rand.org/pubs/research_reports/RRA1645-7.html

Moore, Melinda, Michael A. Wermuth, Laura Werber, Anita Chandra, Darcy Noricks, Adam C. Resnick, Carolyn Chu, and James J. Burks, *Bridging the Gap: Developing a Tool to Support Local Civilian and Military Disaster Preparedness*, RAND Corporation, TR-764-OSD, 2010. As of September 27, 2022: https://www.rand.org/pubs/technical_reports/TR764.html

Moroney, Jennifer D. P., Joe Hogler, Lianne Kennedy-Boudali, and Stephanie Pezard, *Integrating the Full Range of Security Cooperation Programs into Air Force Planning: An Analytic Primer*, RAND Corporation, TR-974-AF, 2011. As of September 27, 2022: https://www.rand.org/pubs/technical_reports/TR974.html

Narayanan, Anu, Debra Knopman, Kristin Van Abel, Benjamin M. Miller, Nicholas E. Burger, Martha Blakely, Alexander D. Rothenberg, Luke Muggy, and Patrick Mills, *Valuing Air Force Electric Power Resilience: A Framework for Mission-Level Investment Prioritization*, RAND Corporation, RR-2771-AF, 2019. As of April 5, 2023: https://www.rand.org/pubs/research_reports/RR2771.html

Narayanan, Anu, Michael J. Lostumbo, Kristin Van Abel, Michael T. Wilson, Anna Jean Wirth, and Rahim Ali, *Grounded: An Enterprise-Wide Look at Department of the Air Force Installation Exposure to Natural Hazards: Implications for Infrastructure Investment Decisionmaking and Continuity of Operations Planning*, RAND Corporation, RR-A523-1, 2021. As of September 27, 2022: https://www.rand.org/pubs/research_reports/RRA523-1.html

National Fire Protection Association, "National Fire Codes Online," homepage, undated. As of September 27, 2022: http://codesonline.nfpa.org

National Fire Protection Association, *NFPA 1144: Standard for Reducing Structure Ignition Hazards from Wildland Fire*, 2018.

National Fire Protection Association, *NFPA 101: Life Safety Code*, 2021.

National Institute of Standards and Technology, *Risk Management Framework for Information Systems and Organizations: A System Life Cycle Approach for Security and Privacy*, Joint Task Force, NIST SP 800-37, revision 2, December 2018.

National Park Service, "National Park System—Units/Parks," webpage, undated-a. As of August 29, 2022:
https://www.nps.gov/aboutus/national-park-system.htm

National Park Service, "Our Mission," webpage, undated-b. As of August 26, 2022:
https://www.nps.gov/aboutus/index.htm

National Park Service, *Planning for a Changing Climate: Climate-Smart Planning and Management in the National Park Service*, 2021.

Naval Facilities Engineering Systems Command, *Climate Change Planning Handbook: Installation Adaptation and Resilience*, January 2017.

New York City Mayor's Office of Resiliency, *Climate Resiliency Design Guidelines*, version 4, September 2020.

NFPA—*See* National Fire Protection Association.

Norris, Fran H., Susan P. Stevens, Betty Pfefferbaum, Karen F. Wyche, and Rose L. Pfefferbaum, "Community Resilience as a Metaphor, Theory, Set of Capacities, and Strategy for Disaster Readiness," *American Journal of Community Psychology*, Vol. 41, Nos. 1–2, 2008.

NPS—*See* National Park Service.

Office of the Deputy Assistant Secretary for Environment, Safety, and Infrastructure, *Micro-Reactor Pilot FAQs*, Department of the Air Force, October 27, 2021.

Office of the Director of Civil Engineers, "Directorate of Civil Engineers Solicits Installation Assistance to Screen for Severe Weather/Climate Hazards on AF Installations," Headquarters, Department of the Air Force, September 3, 2020.

Office of the Under Secretary of Defense for Acquisition and Sustainment, *Report on Effects of a Changing Climate to the Department of Defense*, U.S. Department of Defense, January 2019.

Office of the Undersecretary for Policy for Strategy, Plans, and Capabilities, *Department of Defense Climate Risk Analysis*, U.S. Department of Defense, October 2021.

Paton, Douglas, and David Johnston, "Disasters and Communities: Vulnerability, Resilience and Preparedness," *Disaster Prevention and Management*, Vol. 10, No. 4, 2001.

Peterson, Heather, and Joe Hogler, *Understanding Country Planning: A Guide for Air Force Component Planners*, RAND Corporation, TR-1186-AF, 2012. As of September 27, 2022:
https://www.rand.org/pubs/technical_reports/TR1186.html

Pfefferbaum, Betty J., Dori B. Reissman, Rose L. Pfefferbaum, Richard W. Klomp, and Robin H. Gurwitch, "Building Resilience to Mass Trauma Events," in Lynda S. Doll, Sandra E. Bonzo, David A. Sleet, and James A. Mercy, eds., *Handbook of Injury and Violence Prevention*, Springer, 2006.

Pinson, A. O. and K. D. White, S. A. Moore, S. D. Samuelson, B. A. Thames, P. S. O'Brien, C. A. Hiemstra, P. M. Loechl, and E. E. Ritchie, *Army Climate Resilience Handbook: Change 1*, U.S. Army Corps of Engineers, August 2020.

Pinson, A. O., K. D. White, E. E. Ritchie, H. M. Conners, and J. R. Arnold, *DoD Installation Exposure to Climate Change at Home and Abroad*, U.S. Army Corps of Engineers, April 2021.

Randall, D. A., R. A. Wood, S. Bony, R. Colman, T. Fichefet, J. Fyfe, V. Kattsov, A. Pitman, J. Shukla, J. Srinivasan, R. J. Stouffer, A. Sumi, and K. E. Taylor, "Climate Models and Their Evaluation," in S. Solomon, D. Qin, M. Manning, Z. Chen, M. Marquis, K. B. Averyt, M. Tignor, and H. L. Miller, eds., *Climate Change 2007: The Physical Science Basis*, Cambridge University Press, 2007.

Resilience Alliance, "Key Concepts," webpage, undated. As of April 25, 2023: https://www.resalliance.org/key-concepts

Robbert, Albert A., Lisa M. Harrington, Tara L. Terry, and H. G. Massey, *Air Force Manpower Requirements and Component Mix: A Focus on Agile Combat Support*, RAND Corporation, RR-617-AF, 2014. As of September 26, 2022: https://www.rand.org/pubs/research_reports/RR617.html

Rollins, Matthew G., Brendan C. Ward, Greg Dillon, Sarah Pratt, and Ann Wolf, "Developing the LANDFIRE Fire Regime Data Products," U.S. Department of Agriculture Forest Service Rocky Mountain Research Station, Intermountain Fire Sciences Laboratory, 2007.

Rose, Adam, "Defining and Measuring Economic Resilience to Disasters," *Disaster Prevention and Management*, Vol. 13, No. 4, 2004.

Sawyers, Cheryl, "First Panel Installed at Eglin's Solar Farm," *Air Force News*, January 20, 2017.

Schneider, Jennifer, "Air Force, USFWS Partner to Restore Fish Habitat," *Air Force News*, May 27, 2021.

Scott, Joe H., and Robert E. Burgan, *Standard Fire Behavior Fuel Models: A Comprehensive Set for Use with Rothermel's Surface Fire Spread Model*, U.S. Department of Agriculture, Forest Service, RMRS-GTR-153, 2005.

Seli, Rob C., Stuart Brittan, and Chuck W. McHugh, "FlamMap Online Help, version 6.0," available from within the FlamMap application, 2019.

Sims, Carra S., Chaitra M. Hardison, Kirsten M. Keller, and Abby Robyn, *Air Force Personnel Research: Recommendations for Improved Alignment*, RAND Corporation, RR-814-AF, 2014. As of September 26, 2022:
https://www.rand.org/pubs/research_reports/RR814.html

Sonn, Christopher C., and Adrian T. Fisher, "Sense of Community: Community Resilient Responses to Oppression and Change," *Journal of Community Psychology*, Vol. 26, No. 5, 1998.

Spirtas, Michael, Thomas Young, and S. Rebecca Zimmerman, *What It Takes: Air Force Command of Joint Operations*, RAND Corporation, MG-777-AF, 2009. As of September 27, 2022:
https://www.rand.org/pubs/monographs/MG777.html

Spirtas, Michael, Yool Kim, Frank Camm, Shirley M. Ross, Debra Knopman, Forrest E. Morgan, Sebastian Joon Bae, M. Scott Bond, John S. Crown, and Elaine Simmons, *A Separate Space: Creating a Military Service for Space*, RAND Corporation, RR-4263-AF, 2020. As of September 27, 2022:
https://www.rand.org/pubs/research_reports/RR4263.html

Stancy Correll, Diana, "Travis Air Force Base Orders Evacuations Following LNU Lightning Complex Fire," *Air Force Times*, August 20, 2020.

Tarraf, Danielle C., William Shelton, Edward Parker, Brien Alkire, Diana Gehlhaus Carew, Justin Grana, Alexis Levedahl, Jasmin Léveillé, Jared Mondschein, James Ryseff, Ali Wyne, Dan Elinoff, Edward Geist, Benjamin N. Harris, Eric Hui, Cedric Kenney, Sydne Newberry, Chandler Sachs, Peter Schirmer, Danielle Schlang, Victoria Smith, Abbie Tingstad, Padmaja Vedula, and Kristin Warren, *The Department of Defense Posture for Artificial Intelligence: Assessment and Recommendations*, RAND Corporation, RR-4229-OSD, 2019. As of September 27, 2022:
https://www.rand.org/pubs/research_reports/RR4229.html

Technical Manual 5-803-01, *Installation Master Planning*, U.S. Army Corps of Engineers, June 13, 1986.

Technical Manual 5-803-14, *Site Planning and Design*, U.S. Army Corps of Engineers, October 14, 1994.

Thaler, David E., Gary Cecchine, Anny Wong, and Timothy Jackson, *Building Partner Health Capacity with U.S. Military Forces: Enhancing AFSOC Health Engagement Missions*, RAND Corporation, TR-1201-AF, 2012. As of September 27, 2022:
https://www.rand.org/pubs/technical_reports/TR1201.html

TM—*See* Technical Manual.

UFC—*See* Unified Facilities Criteria.

Unified Facilities Criteria 1-200-01, *DoD Building Code*, U.S. Department of Defense, 2002–2020.

Unified Facilities Criteria 1-200-02, *High Performance and Sustainable Building Requirements, with Change 2*, U.S. Department of Defense, December 1, 2020.

Unified Facilities Criteria 2-100-01, *Installation Master Planning*, U.S. Department of Defense, September 30, 2020, change 1, April 8, 2022.

Unified Facilities Criteria 3-201, *Civil Engineering*, U.S. Department of Defense, April 1, 2018, change 1, April 1, 2021.

Unified Facilities Criteria 3-201-01, *Civil Engineering*, U.S. Department of Defense, December 20, 2022.

Unified Facilities Criteria 3-201-02, *Landscape Architecture*, U.S. Department of Defense, April 29, 2020, change 1, February 9, 2021.

Unified Facilities Criteria 3-210-06A, *Site Planning and Design*, U.S. Department of Defense, January 1, 2006 (replaced by UFC 3-201-01).

Unified Facilities Criteria 3-301-01, *Structural Engineering*, U.S. Department of Defense, April 11, 2023.

Unified Facilities Criteria 3-400-02, *Design: Engineering Weather Data*, U.S. Department of Defense, September 20, 2018.

Unified Facilities Criteria 3-600-01, *Fire Protection Engineering for Facilities*, U.S. Department of Defense, updated September 26, 2006.

U.S. Air Force, *Strategic Posture Annex to the USAF Strategic Master Plan*, May 2015.

U.S. Army, *Army Installations Strategy Implementation Plan Fiscal Years 2022–2024*, undated.

U.S. Army Corps of Engineers, "DD1391 Processor System," fact sheet, updated July 28, 2022.

U.S. Climate Resilience Tool, "Department of Defense Regional Sea Level (DRSL) Database," webpage, last modified February 27, 2021. As of May 31, 2023: https://toolkit.climate.gov/tool/department-defense-regional-sea-level-drsl-database

U.S. Code, Title 10, Armed Forces; Subtitle A, General Military Law; Part IV, Service, Supply, and Procurement; Chapter 169, Military Construction and Military Family Housing; Subchapter III, Administration of Military Construction and Military Family Housing; Section 2864, Master Plans for Major Military Installations.

U.S. Department of Defense, "DOD Announces Installation Climate Exposure Assessments Plan Through the Defense Climate Assessment Tool," news release, April 22, 2021.

U.S. Department of Defense, *Department of Defense Climate Adaptation Plan*, September 1, 2021.

USGCRP—*See* U.S. Global Change Research Program.

U.S. Geological Survey and U.S. Forest Service, "Fire Occurrence Dataset, 1984-2021, Monitoring Trends in Burn Severity (MTBS) Program," 2021.

U.S. Global Change Research Program, *Climate Science Special Report: Fourth National Climate Assessment*, Vol. I, 2017.

U.S. Global Change Research Program, "Overview," *Fourth National Climate Assessment Impacts, Risks, and Adaptation in the United States*, Vol. II, 2018.

U.S. Government Accountability Office, *Climate Resilience: A Strategic Investment Approach for High-Priority Projects Could Help Target Federal Resources*, October 23, 2019.

U.S. Senate, "Military Infrastructure and Climate Resilience," hearing before the Subcommittee on Military Construction, Veterans Affairs, and Related Agencies, May 19, 2021.

Vasquez, Richard B., "Audit of Climate Change Adaptation and Facility Resilience at Military Installations in California," memorandum, December 6, 2021.

Wagner, Amy, "Langley Construction FONPA Announcement," Joint Base Langley-Eustis News, July 18, 2011.

Weilant, Sarah, Aaron Strong, and Benjamin M. Miller, *Incorporating Resilience into Transportation Planning and Assessment*, RAND Corporation, RR-3038-TRB, 2019. As of September 26, 2022:
https://www.rand.org/pubs/research_reports/RR3038.html

Weniger, Russell, "Setting Priorities: Tactical MDI Aligns Facilities to Mission," *Air Force Civil Engineer*, Vol. 26, No. 1, 2018.

Wieser-Willson, Amy, "FLOOD NEWS: Guardsmen Install Flood Barrier Never Before Used in Fargo," *Air Force News*, March 17, 2010.

Wilson, Heather, and David L. Goldfein, "United States Air Force Infrastructure Investment Strategy," memorandum for record, Department of the Air Force, January 29, 2019.

'IK
oup UK Ltd.
ö1123
00007B/26

Milton Keynes UK
Ingram Content Group UK Ltd.
UKHW050639161123
432680UK00007B/26